Advance Praise for the Book

'Wodehouse comes to India's MBA-land. *Been There Bungled That* is a brilliantly irrepressible look at the "classic engineer-MBA's" journey through corporate land. Amazing how an insider has provided an insightful and delightful outside-in perspective on our foibles in consultancy, marketing, advertising and banking. The result is a roll on the floor laughter narrative. A must read for all corporate types who take themselves seriously.'—**Vikram Sakhuja, CEO, Maxus Worldwide**

'A really funny look at corporations, travel, family, and life in general.'—**Arvind Sharma, Chairman & CEO, Leo Burnett India Subcontinent**

'A hilarious book. Among other things, Paddy captures the inherent humour in a marketing job brilliantly.'—**Jayant Kapur, ex-Chairman, Bacardi Martini India Ltd**

'I've spent my entire career in the advertising industry and have loved it. But till I read this book, I didn't realize how comical it can be from time to time!'—**Sam Balsara, Chairman & Managing Director, Madison World**

'If you take your job seriously, you must read this book because Paddy gives you numerous hilarious reasons why you should not!'—**Shantanu Khosla, Managing Director, Procter & Gamble India**

BEEN THERE BUNGLED THAT

AT COLLEGE, CONSULTING, MARKETING, ADVERTISING, AND LIFE

PADDY RANGAPPA

EBURY PRESS

An imprint of Penguin Random House

EBURY PRESS

USA | Canada | UK | Ireland | Australia
New Zealand | India | South Africa | China | Singapore

Ebury Press is part of the Penguin Random House group of companies whose addresses can be found at global.penguinrandomhouse.com

Published by Penguin Random House India Pvt. Ltd
4th Floor, Capital Tower 1, MG Road,
Gurugram 122 002, Haryana, India

Penguin Random House India

First published by Random House India 2011

10 9 8 7 6 5 4 3 2

ISBN 9788184004335

Typeset in Berling by Pen2print Media Solution, Okhla

Printed at Repro India Limited

www.penguin.co.in

MIX
Paper from responsible sources
FSC® C047271

This is a legitimate digitally printed version of the book and therefore might not have certain extra finishing on the cover.

Contents

Dissuaded from doing an MBA 1
The mechanical engineer 6
Campus life 9
Married to the brand 12
Meeting more brand managers 17
A meaningful summer internship 20
Grappling with the IIMA curriculum 22
Submitting the POM report... and meeting someone 25
Discussing career with Dr Wakefield (again) 30
A heavenly auto ride 33
The MBA man turns to consultancy 39
Parents meeting parents 42
Hurtling towards the wedding 46
The consultant 48
Tying the knot 51
The sophisticated shopper 54
Getting the first consultancy project 58
The dynamic, supercharged, recently-trained executive 61

The known unknowns	65
A man's monthly syndrome	69
Difficult conversations	72
Rekindling of an old love	76
The decisive, purposeful executive	80
A productive railway journey	83
A rollercoaster bus ride	87
The unique work ethic of Kerala	90
A banana or two a day	94
An angel joins the family	98
Driving the angel to sleep	103
Getting the full hotel service	107
'How long will it take to get there?'	110
An electric guitar for children	113
Addressing a change	117
An ancient civilization in the 21st century	121
The professional tennis player	124
A sensible sense of time	127
The dual-country driver	130
A king-sized city	133
The traits of a successful copy writer	137
Talk in America as Americans do	142
Flying travails	146
The disease that is mobile	150
Reunion with Q&P Mumbai	154

Preparing for a pitch 157
A fraternity of fatness 160
The stranger danger 163
The after-pitch effect 168
Devious inanimate objects 171
Fridge, oh glorious fridge 175
The EE's and SS's of marketing at Gronollers 179
Supermarket man 184
Close encounters of the durian kind 187
Laundry Immersion Day 190
Helping out with homework 193
Mobile love 196
The power of branding 199
Something attempted, something done 202
Haircut evolution 205
Branding bliss 208
For the record 213
Taking marketing to the bank 216
Medically speaking 221
Banking on money 225
Culture shock in Tokyo 229
Taking taxi trips in Tokyo 233
The quest for a new toilet seat 236
We don't tolerate conflict of interest here 239
The flying go-getter gets going 243

The two secrets of marriage compatibility 247
A doctor for daughter 251
Lost in transportation 255
Avoiding the Goldman Sachs blunder 259
Fanatic football fever 264
The intrepid explorer 267
Exiting the bank 270
Hubby the handyman 274
The guilty party 279
Been there, done that 283
A Note on the Author 288

Dissuaded from doing an MBA

It is not often that a casual conversation with a relative stranger can have a significant impact on one's life but it happened to me when I spoke with Dr Sidelinger Wakefield in my third year of engineering.

I was home from college for the summer break and Dr Wakefield, my father's friend, was visiting. He was on holiday from the US, where he was a professor in an institution with a very amusing name: Brown University. I remember wondering whether the US was littered with sister universities bearing the names of other colours like Blue University, Green University and, perhaps exclusively for women, Pink University.

'So Jags—,' my name is Jagannath Srinivasan but people call me Jags '—what are your plans after engineering?' asked Wakefield, as he joined the family for tea one evening.

'I'm taking the CAT,' I said.

'Which cat?' The professor looked around him in confusion, as if expecting to see one slinking around. 'And where are you taking it?'

'Not the animal,' I explained. 'I'm taking the Common Admissions Test to get into the IIMs.' The professor continued to look stumped. 'The Indian Institutes of Management. To get an MBA. That's Master of…'

'At least I know what an MBA is!' said Wakefield. 'But why an MBA?'

I was puzzled by the question. 'I'm puzzled by the question,' I said. 'What do you mean?'

'You're studying engineering now, right?' I nodded. 'Why?'

'That's easy,' I said. 'I passed the JEE—the Joint Entrance Exam—to get into IIT. That's Indian Institute of Technology. I did badly in the medical college entrance test.'

'What?! You actually wanted to be a doctor?'

'Of course not,' I said. 'Why do you ask?'

'Because you took the medical college entrance test. You just told me!' The professor was getting agitated and his voice was rising.

'Yes, I did,' I replied soothingly. 'But that was only as a back-up. I was not serious.'

The professor shook his head in bewilderment. 'Ok, so you really wanted to do engineering but just for fun, took the medical college test too. I understand—or at least I think I do—so tell me: what engineering are you studying?'

'Mechanical engineering at IIT Kanpur.'

'Why?'

'With my rank in the JEE—the Joint Entrance Exam,' I said a little sheepishly, 'that was the best I could get. But it's a great university. In the overall ratings...'

'No! I mean why did you choose mechanical engineering?'

'I didn't. I chose electronics engineering but could only get IIT Kharagpur for electronics. Mechanical engineering at Kanpur is better than electronics engineering at Kharagpur.'

'Now I'm puzzled,' said the professor. 'Better in what way?'

'In ranking of course,' I said. I wondered how this gentleman had become a professor. He seemed to be lacking basic intelligence.

'Let me get this straight. You chose your area of specialization based on its relative popularity and the popularity of the institute?'

'Yes, but it's not just the relative popularity of the specialization and the institute separately. It's the *combination* that's important. For example mechanical engineering at Kanpur is better than electrical engineering at Kharagpur but civil engineering in Kharagpur is better than electrical engineering in Madras. It's very complicated,' I said smugly. ('And therefore beyond your comprehension,' I added, but only to myself.)

'I'm not going to try to follow that,' said Wakefield. ('Exactly,' I said, again to myself.) 'Let me come back to my first question. Why, after studying mechanical engineering, do you want to do an MBA straightaway?'

'Well, I'm just taking the CAT, as I said, but I'll also be applying for some engineering jobs on campus...'—the professor began to nod with enthusiasm—'... as well as applying for an MS degree in the US. Also...'

The professor stopped nodding with enthusiasm and interrupted me. 'Hang on. You don't know whether you'll work or do an MBA or study for an MS?'

I nodded. 'It depends on what I get.'

'This is nonsense!' The professor was getting excited again, I could tell, because his voice was rising once more. 'You need to know what you want to do in life.'

He then began a lecture of an esoteric nature, covering how I should view education as preparatory ground for my long-term career; how I should apply what I study to the real world; by doing this, how I should attain a passion

'Mechanical engineering at Kanpur is better than electrical engineering at Kharagpur but civil engineering in Kharagpur is better than electrical engineering in Madras. It's very complicated.'

for my profession; and using this experience, how I should figure out if I would like to study further; and if so, in what field.

'Go get a job with an engineering company,' he said finally. 'Work there for a couple of years. Then figure out if you want to continue working, or do an MBA... or specialize further in engineering.'

Mm, this professor was not so nutty after all. My parents were definitely impressed: both were listening wide-eyed and nodding sagely. Even my younger sister seemed to be nodding sagely but that might have been in response to the rock music faintly audible from a neighbour's radio.

'Ok,' I said.

'Splendid!' said the professor. 'And that means don't waste your time chasing cats this winter!'

We all laughed politely.

The mechanical engineer

IN ACCORDANCE WITH THE COUNSEL I had received from the learned professor Wakefield, I only applied for jobs on campus in my final year. Around me, classmates were applying for the CAT with gusto and filling out forms to take the Graduate Records Examination (GRE) to gain entrance into US universities, but I ignored them.

The job application process began with a group discussion, where a few of us sat together and debated grave topics like *Is urbanization in India's interest?* and *The role of women in modern society* under the watchful eye of the company executive. I don't remember what we said and how meaningful it was but I remember the difficulty of talking formally to a bunch of chums I had lived with for four years in close proximity. I mean, the guy sitting next to me (looking ridiculous in a tie that he was wearing for the first time in his life) was the same man who, out of economic necessity, regularly split a cup of tea with me (and equally regularly argued that I had given him less than his rightful 50 percent). It was tough to keep a straight face and address him thus: 'Sorry, Mr Ramkumar, I would like to point out a flaw in your argument,' when the inclination was to say: 'Stop talking rot, you ass!'

The group discussions were followed by interviews, which were followed by more group discussions, where I met the same people and sometimes debated the same topics. The whole process was tedious but at the end of it, I had something to show: a job as Graduate Engineer Trainee (GET) at Kasiram Motors, one of India's leading automobile manufacturers.

Soon after graduating, I joined Kasiram Motors in their factory in Pune along with a bunch of engineering graduates like me from across India. As GETs we were rotated through various departments so we would learn the ropes of this gigantic automobile company. I spent a few weeks each in the forge, the design centre, the assembly line and other such exotic places and realized I had not found my calling in life. The forge—despite its intense heat—left me cold; my pulse did not rise at the design centre, where I observed brainy engineers peering into the insides of internal combustion engines trying to enhance their power while reducing their fuel consumption. And after spending ten minutes on the assembly line—where the vehicle inches along gradually getting built by an army of workers feverishly attaching things like wheels, cam shaft, and gear box to it—I was bored.

'What happened, Mr Srinivasan?' asked the supervisor as he observed me trying—unsuccessfully—to stifle a yawn. 'Are we boring you here?'

'Well, sir, it *is* a bit repetitive, you know,' I said. 'I've been standing here for 15 minutes watching the same worker fit the same wheel in the exact same place on the same type of truck about 40 times.'

'Oh, maybe you would like us to enhance the entertainment? Perhaps we should ask the workers to do a little dance for you?'

'Not a dance, sir; that would be unnecessary. But if they could mix things up a bit here, it would...' I stopped because I suddenly got the suspicion, as I observed my fellow GETs laughing, that he was being sarcastic.

After a year I discovered with passion that I had not yet discovered my career passion. I knew with certainty that I was not cut out for an engineering job.

Campus life

So a few months later, I took the CAT and was pleased to get a call for an interview at the Indian Institute of Management, Ahmedabad (IIMA). Similar to the job applications after engineering, here too the process began with a group discussion. But this time we did not know each other. As we sat in the waiting room, fidgeting nervously but trying to look calm and managerial, a young IIMA professor entered the room. He wore a smart suit and had a thin leather folder tucked neatly under his arm.

'Good morning,' he announced to the room at large; then he removed a notebook from his leather folder, placed the folder on a seat and walked around introducing himself to all the candidates. 'Hi, I'm Rahul Ghai.' He then shook hands with each candidate and, when they spoke, noted their name in his notebook. As he finished going through all the candidates, a door on the other side of the room opened and we were invited inside.

I was surprised when Ghai walked into the room and sat down with us, instead of going to the head of the table, where a lady in a crisp cotton sari was already seated. She gave us the topic. That's when we all realized that Ghai was a candidate like us. But unlike us, he knew everyone's name and dominated the group discussion by addressing everyone personally: 'Good point, Ms Anjali Kumar', 'I wouldn't go quite as far as that, Mr Bharadwaj' and 'Sorry, Mr Srinivasan, I disagree with you.'

Needless to say, Ghai made it to the final interview and was finally selected. Luckily, so was I.

Life on IIMA was fun, I suppose, if you ignored the curriculum. But I found it difficult to ignore a curriculum that occupied every waking hour of my life. No, correct that. I even dreamt about the curriculum when I slept: for example, after a particularly taxing class on operations management, I remember dreaming about Lorenz curves for Pareto distributions and waking up muttering '80-20, 80-20'.

During the classes, the lecturers did not refer to any text book, which in itself could have been a fantastic approach to teaching if they did not expect students to refer to it either. But they did. 'You have to read the textbooks at our own leisure,' they would say with a straight face, even though everyone knew there was no concept of one's own—or even somebody else's borrowed—leisure at IIMA.

Instead they would spend the entire lecture time discussing a case. The IIMA professor considers the case the backbone of the MBA program. The IIMA student, who is expected to analyse three or four cases daily, each 50-100 pages long, considers it the bane of the MBA program. The cases, were written well—some droll, others fast-paced and a few like introspective memoirs—but our reading pleasure usually stopped at the third page and did not return during the next 38 pages of prose and the further 20 pages of appendices filled with statistics.

The students' job was to analyse the case—sometimes alone, sometimes in a group—and talk about it in the class. The professors' job was to make sarcastic, biting remarks about everything the student said.

'So who would like to present their analysis of the MacMillan and Forbisher case?' the professor asked. I raised my hand.

'Ok, Srinivasan, go,' he said.

I spoke eloquently for five minutes.

'So?' the professor said, his eyebrows raised, when I finished.

'Sorry, sir,' I said. 'What do you mean by "so"?'

'I mean what is your analysis?'

'That *is* my analysis, sir. I just gave it to you,' I said. ('Weren't you listening?' I wanted to add.)

'That was not an analysis. That was a mere repetition of case facts that you've wasted five minutes of our class time on. Who else would like to…'

Why would anyone volunteer to speak and get their argument torn to bits? Well, you had to speak to get marks for class participation, a significant portion of your assessment. So we raised our hands and we spoke; we listened to the professors acerbic comments and then we spoke; when someone made a point we disagreed with, we spoke; and if someone said something we agreed with, we spoke. It is at IIMA that future managers learn to talk when they have nothing to say—a trait that will serve them well throughout their careers.

Married to the brand

As I entered the headquarters of Gronollers on the first day of my summer internship, I was as excited as a child on her first visit to the circus. After all, Gronollers was the famous multinational company known for its wonderful brands: creams that make women look younger as they grow older; ointments that, when spread on the chest of a child with a chronic cold and cough, enable him to sleep peacefully and wake up with a clear chest (and a hug for his miracle-performing mother); soaps that clean the body *and* brighten the soul; and many others.

At the centre of Gronollers are its wonderful brand managers. Brand managers are the essence of humanity, the pride of civilization, the salt of the earth. These amazing creatures from the dreamy world of marketing bring all their abundant energy to bear on the brands they manage.

I was thrilled when I was told my internship would be on Swipe, Gronollers's leading detergent brand and that I would work under its brand manager, Ashutosh Ojha. As I entered Ojha's hallowed office, I felt a sense of awe, exhilaration and apprehension, all rolled into one, exactly the maelstrom of emotions I felt when, as a boy of ten, I had first glimpsed the Taj Mahal.

Ojha was an intense man in his early thirties, with curly hair and a short moustache that heightened his air of seriousness. He nodded briskly and pointed to the chair in front of his desk. I sat down.

'Swipe is a billion dollar brand and a jewel in Gronollers's crown,' said Ojha sternly, 'Do you know how important the detergent category is to the company? You could say that detergents—and especially Swipe—are the heartbeat of Gronollers.'

I was impressed. But I was also ashamed to admit (only to myself) that before that day, I had not thought about detergents seriously. Yes, I had used them to wash my clothes—peer pressure at college had often forced me to do this—but I had done so without delving into their inner meaning.

'What does the Swipe detergent brand do?' Ojha asked suddenly.

'Washes clothes?' I ventured.

Ojha snorted. 'That's like asking you what you do and you replying, "I breathe".'

His curly hair shook when he was excited, which happened when he talked about Swipe. Since he talked about little else, his hair bobbed up and down almost continuously. He was passionate about every aspect of the brand. With glistening eyes, he related Swipe's rich history: how it had conquered millions of hearts in country after country before making its tumultuous entry into the Indian market. Pinned at eye-level on a board in front of his desk was the Swipe Brand Manifesto—a noble statement describing Swipe's function in this world, its personality and how it behaves in a crisis.

His two-hour presentation included testimonials from delighted Swipe consumers; charts showing Swipe's

'Swipe washes clothes? That's like asking you what you do and you replying, "I breathe".'

performance over the years, across the 26 states, in hard and soft water and among people of varying educational qualifications; quotations by senior company officers (like '*When times are good, invest in marketing Swipe; when times are bad, invest more*'); and numerous advertisements used to promote the brand. I soon understood why washing clothes merely scratched the surface of Swipe's resume. The brand does much, much more. It brightens your outlook on life; facilitates your career progression; smoothens your rocky marriage; and enables your children to excel in school, in not just academics, but also painting, debating, and medium-distance bicycling.

However, it appeared that a dark villain was intent on thwarting Swipe's honourable charter. This was the local competitor's brand, Seema.

'Did you know,' said Ojha in a quivering voice, 'that Seema uses more sodium sulphate in its product than any other detergent in India?'

I shook my head.

'Sodium sulphate is a filler that adds volume to the product without contributing to cleaning. Yet these rascals have loaded Seema with it... How low can they stoop? But we're working on a new ad campaign showing how a young mother goes astray in bringing up her children by switching to a cheap detergent with excess sodium sulphate; her child—the class monitor—gets reprimanded by the teacher for the first time in his life. The mother immediately realizes the error of her ways. The last scene shows her hugging her son with one hand as he wins a medal for javelin-throw, while holding up a package of Swipe in her other hand. Anyway, let's discuss your assignment now.'

I leaned forward eagerly. 'Will I be working on this new ad campaign?'

'Of course not!' said Ojha. 'Only assistant brand managers and upwards get involved in the advertising. You need to first understand the brand and the category thoroughly. Here—' he reached behind him for four fat binders each the size of the Mumbai yellow pages '—are the recent ORG reports. Dig into them. Analyse detergent performance by pack size across urban and rural India. Pay special attention to the coastal areas and hilly regions. And then—' he gave me three box files, thick as sumo wrestlers' arms '—analyse these consumer reports.'

I nodded enthusiastically. It sounded like work that was meaningful and thrilling at the same time. Once again I congratulated myself for quitting a job in a company that merely designed internal combustion engines and built trucks and doing an MBA. Now I could do some real work.

Meeting more brand managers

ON THE FIRST FRIDAY OF my internship, I got invited to a party by my boss.

'It's just a few college friends coming home,' said Ojha. 'You'll meet brand managers from other companies. And you can help me serve the drinks and so on.'

I was ecstatic. A chance to meet more marketing people from other companies, share drinks with them, quiz them about their brands... What more could an intern ask for?

Ojha, still single, lived in an elegant apartment in Juhu, with one bedroom and a large hall-cum-dining area. At the party, I met brand managers as zealous as Ojha. As I helped Ojha serve the drinks, I encountered the raw passion of a brand manager for his brand.

'What will you drink?' I asked a tall man in his thirties. 'Can I get you a rum and Coke?'

He raised an eyebrow and said, 'I am the brand manager of Pepsi.'

'Pleased to meet you,' I said and similarly introduced myself. 'Now coming back to your drink...?'

He raised both eyebrows this time, so much that they almost disappeared into his hairline.

'I mean,' he said coldly, 'that I don't drink Coke. Never have. Never will.'

After dinner (pizza delivery), a couple of the guests helped make some tea and coffee. I was seated next to a vase filled with fresh flowers that someone had brought for Ojha.

'These roses,' I said as I took a sip of tea, 'Delightful fragrance.'

'No!' snapped the woman on my right. I jumped with shock, not expecting my innocuous remark to draw such an angry response, especially from this woman who had exhibited a mild-mannered temperament throughout the party. She continued vehemently: 'And awful taste too.'

I was puzzled. 'Have you been eating these flowers?' I said and examined the bunch for bite marks.

'Oh you mean the roses in the vase?' said the woman, sounding contrite, 'Sorry'.

Apparently she had thought I was referring to the tea, in particular the *Three Roses* brand and, as brand manager of its rival, had instinctively taken umbrage.

Another guest at the party was a brand manager in a cigarette company. I wandered over to him and asked how things were.

'Great!' he said. He went on to rave about the terrific brand he managed, how its tobacco leaves were procured (apparently very carefully), the technology that went into the manufacture of its filter (which included the use of some formidable glue) and the elegant manner it was distributed (in neat cardboard boxes).

'But tell me,' I said, 'what about the recent movement to quit smoking and the increasing medical evidence that cigarettes are harmful to health? How has that affected your brand?'

'It's like any other industry,' said the tobacco man, 'you take advantage of every positive opportunity and you minimize the impact of any bad news.'

'By bad news, you mean the fact that people are realizing that cigarettes can kill?'

'Yes, what else?' he asked. He appeared genuinely puzzled by my question.

A meaningful summer internship

AFTER MEETING A BUNCH OF brand managers as committed to the welfare of their brand as my boss Ashutosh Ojha, I came back to my desk at Gronollers with renewed fire in my belly.

'I've got an important project for you,' Ojha announced grandly. 'The competitor Seema is available in one-rupee sachets and it is very popular. We introduced the Swipe sachet priced at two rupees recently. But for some reason it is not doing as well. I want you to tell us why.'

I thought I already knew the answer but Ojha was still speaking.

'From your analysis of the ORG reports,' he said, 'peer into the monthly sales performance of the small pack sizes in small and big towns. Re-read the consumer reports. Then spend a few days observing consumers as they buy detergent in kirana stores and supermarkets; then talk to them. Find out what else they buy at the same time—and why? What is their underlying motivation? How do they feel after the purchase? And as you do this…'

In the following days, I chewed the ORG data raw and could recite the market share of key detergent pack sizes for the past three quarters to the first decimal place. I pored over Swipe consumer research to learn who used it, what they earned and what they thought about violence in films. I explored supermarkets and kirana stores, enthusiastically interviewing women about their detergent behaviour... but not always getting enthusiastic responses.

'Hello, Ma'am,' I said to a woman in her forties as she emerged from the supermarket with a bag of her purchases in one hand (the 2 kilogram Swipe package was clearly visible through the plastic) and a sulking child in the other. 'I notice that you've purchased Swipe detergent. Excellent! Can you tell me what you're feeling right now with that pack in your hand?'

'Tired,' snapped the woman. 'I've carried this heavy bag for the past fifteen minutes while trying to hold on to this boy at the same time.'

'Yes, of course,' I said. 'But I'm asking about your emotional state. Do you feel a sense of accomplishment and tranquillity, as if you've just enjoyed a sauna bath?'

'Are you mad?' she snapped. 'Do I look tranquil? Now please get out of my way.'

I retreated, unfazed, and lurked near the cashier looking for the next shopper with Swipe.

At the end of my internship, I was convinced that marketing was my calling. I returned to IIMA in a state of bliss.

Grappling with the IIMA curriculum

I FOUND TWO COURSES PARTICULARLY PAINFUL at IIMA: mathematics and statistics for management (MSM) and productions and operations management (POM). *All* the courses were difficult of course, but in theory, I ought to have found MSM and POM easy.

I had done well in mathematics in school and it was at the root of many of my engineering subjects, like thermodynamics and fluid mechanics; so MSM should have been a breeze. My first MSM quiz had 20 questions, all with multiple answers. I attacked them like a veteran mathematician, crunching numbers, finding my answer among the choices, circling it and moving on.

I thought I had answered all the questions correctly but I was prepared to get one answer wrong. However I did not get one question wrong—I got seventeen. The diabolical professor had anticipated each mistake I could make and included that answer among the alternatives. It was heartening to see most of the class reeling under a similar shock but there were half a dozen killjoys who had got the full 20 marks out of 20.

POM should have been a breeze *and* a cakewalk for me as I had cemented my engineering degree with two years of working on the manufacturing floor, but it wasn't. I remember the terrible shock of getting a 'D' in my first POM quiz. Then I brightened up thinking that if an accomplished engineer and automobile whiz could manage only a 'D', how miserably the arts students would have fared. I turned to my neighbour Aarti Sengupta, a literature graduate from Stella Maris, Chennai.

'Wow! Was that a killer quiz or what? What did you get?'

'An 'A',' she said and showed me her paper. 'You?'

With an abrupt 'Excuse me, Ram is calling me from the door—I'll catch you later,' I left her and moved quickly towards the vast outdoors.

If POM1 was difficult, POM2 was heart-rending. The quizzes were bad enough but the detailed reports we had to submit were worse. I remember one report—an analysis of the case *The Problem of Optimizing Production at Extraordinary Motors, Ranchi*—we had to submit by 5 pm on the upcoming Monday evening. Given my lacklustre performance in the course so far, I hoped to submit a decent report and get at least a 'C'. But unfortunately I couldn't get much done that weekend because it was particularly busy: we had our inter-dormitory tennis tournament, followed by a dormitory party and the movie *Ram Teri Ganga Maili* had just been released and therefore had to be seen.

Any professor with an iota of compassion would recognize that the circumstances were extenuating and therefore extend the deadline but not our POM professor Balakrishnan Thampi, a hard-hearted man from Kerala who habitually chewed glass and scowled at infants. So modifying my goal to submitting *something* and avoiding an 'F', I skipped breakfast, classes and lunch and wrote feverishly. By 4 pm I was about three-fourths done. Just one hour to go! I put my head down and wrote even faster, looking neither left nor right. Finally I was done. As I stapled the pages together I looked at my watch. Oh, no! It was 5.35 pm. I sprinted from the dorm with my report and, in reaching the administration building at 5.41 pm, probably set a new world record. But it didn't matter.

'POM2 report for Thampi?' asked the research assistant in a bored voice. 'Sorry, you're 45 minutes late—' she was lying: I was only 41 minutes late '—and the professor has already taken the reports home. Better luck next time,' she added, stifling a yawn.

I stood there with my mouth open for a few moments; then walked away in a daze.

Submitting the POM report... and meeting someone

I CONTINUED WALKING IN A DAZE towards the front gate. I was appalled. My average grade in this subject was already precariously poised; an 'F' would surely send it hurtling over the cliff of ignominy. Looking for some small succour to reduce my sorrow, I ordered tea at Soma's at the front gate and sat alone, brooding, for half an hour. Then my friend Umesh Goregaonkar walked over. I ordered another cup of tea and told him what happened. Unlike the research assistant, he expressed deep sympathy. Then he had an idea.

'Why don't you go to the professor's house and try to give it to him? It's unlikely that the monster will relent but there's no harm in trying.'

I knew where Prof. Thampi stayed in the staff quarters on campus because I had passed his house once on a walk. So I walked there now, practising what I would say ('sir, it was a very important tennis match and since my body was stiff from the previous match, I had to first get a massage by my dorm-mates. After the match I was so tired I slept for 12 hours straight...' I thought it would be judicious not to mention the party or *Ram Teri Ganga Maili*).

It was 7.30 pm when I reached the professor's house—a graceful single-storey structure with a small compound. Everything was quiet and, except for a light in the living room, dark. The garage at the end of the driveway was empty. The professor was obviously out for the evening in his red Maruti. I walked into the open gate and towards the front door, wondering whether I should ring the bell, when I saw that the door was wide open. Standing at its threshold I could see into the living room—a sofa set, coffee table, a cupboard with some curios and beyond that the family dining table on which there was a pile of papers that looked like a bunch of reports...

The POM2 reports! There they were, a few tantalizing feet in front of me. All I had to do was walk up to the table, place my report inside the pile and walk out again. I looked behind me—there was no one on the street. I poked my head into the house. The living room was empty. I took a gingerly step inside. Now I was inside the professor's house; in other words I had already crossed the line of the law, so I walked briskly to the dining table and looked at the top paper on the pile. I was right—it *was* my classmates' reports for this project. In my eagerness to add my report to the pile, I dropped it. As I bent to pick it up, a feminine voice spoke.

'Yes? Can I help you?'

I jumped in shock. Standing in the open door was a tall fair girl, drying her hair with a towel and looking at me quizzically.

'Sorry!' I said, 'I didn't know anyone was at home.'

'Oh,' she said, 'Is that why you entered?'

'Yes,' I said; then realized that it didn't sound right. 'I mean no! That's not why I entered. I am one of Professor's students and I came to ask him something.'

'And?'

'And,' I continued, thinking desperately on my feet, 'since he is obviously not at home, I thought I would leave a note.'

'Oh,' she said with a twinkle in her eye, 'Is that the note in your hand?'

'No!' I clutched my report close to my chest. 'It's ok. I'll meet him tomorrow at class.'

'I'll get you a paper and pen,' she said sweetly. 'You can write your note.'

'No, please. It's ok,' I pleaded. 'I'll leave now. I'm getting late for dinner.'

'I'll tell my father you came,' she said. 'What's your name?'

'Rahul Ghai.' I blurted out the first name that came to my mind—but Ghai was my classmate and another student of Prof. Thampi's class. How stupid of me to drag him into the mess!

'Ok, Mr Ghai,' she said, 'I'll tell my father you came.' Then, seeing me standing there staring at her, she continued: 'Is there anything else?'

'Ganapathi Venkateswariya,' I said, thinking up a fictitious name on my second try. 'That's my name. Sorry.'

'Ganapathi Venkateswariya?' The corners of her mouth were twitching as if she were controlling a major emotion stirring inside. I feared she was about to explode in anger. 'That's your name?' I nodded. 'Not Rahul Ghai?' I shook my head. 'Are you sure?'

'Yes!' I said. 'I'm quite sure. You see Rahul Ghai is my classmate and by mistake...'

'... you thought you were him?' she said and exploded... in laughter. I was relieved that she was taking it so well but also puzzled at what she found so amusing.

'Ok, I'll make a move then,' I said. 'The mess will close.'

'Sure, Mr Venkateswariya,' she said, still giggling. 'You make a move, Mr Venkateswariya. I don't want you to miss your dinner, Mr Venkateswariya.'

I wondered if the poor girl was suffering from some kind of speech problem that made her repeat things. It was a pity because she was pretty and nice and smart and charming and... Shaking myself out of these irrelevant thoughts, I turned to the door.

'Excuse me, Mr Venkateswariya,' she said. I turned back. Now what? 'Since you've come all the way here, would you like to give me the POM2 report you're carrying in your hand?' My jaw dropped. 'I can add it to the pile there and my father will never know.'

Speechlessly, I handed the report to her. She looked briefly at the top page; then, taking a big chunk of the reports out of the pile, placed mine in the middle and replaced the pile on top.

'There,' she said. 'Your report is in the middle somewhere, as if you had submitted it with all the others.'

'Thank you!' I said. 'Thank you very much! You see, I had a very important tennis match over the weekend and since my body was stiff from the previous match, I had to...'

'That's ok, Mr Venkateswariya,' she interrupted me. 'You don't have to explain, Mr Venkateswariya.'

'Ok, then I'll take your leave,' I said. 'Thanks once again. You're an angel.'

I turned red in embarrassment. I hadn't meant to say that—it just came out. I mean I did think that she was an angel—and a charming one at that—but I didn't quite mean to tell her that.

She didn't notice my embarrassment. In fact, she seemed embarrassed herself.

'Thank you,' she said. 'Very sweet of you to say that, Mr Venkateswariya.' I was turning to leave when she added, 'Or should I call you Mr Jagannath Srinivasan?'

I stopped turning. She was smiling. Giving her a sheepish grin, I said: 'Just call me Jags. That's what all my friends call me. And surely,'—once again words were coming out involuntarily from my mouth—'after today's episode, I can consider you a friend?'

'Yes, I think you can,' she said. I turned to leave for the fourth time.

'But,' she continued and I turned back for the fourth time, 'if you consider me a friend, perhaps you'd like to also know my name?' I nodded dumbly. 'Don't worry, I'm going to give you only one—my real name. It's Vidya Thampi.'

Discussing career with Dr Wakefield (again)

'EVERYTHING IS HUNKY DORY,' I said. 'I finished a very good summer internship at Gronollers and I enjoyed working in marketing.'

I was at home for a brief vacation before heading back to IIMA. My father's friend Professor Sidelinger Wakefield—yes, the same professor who had dissuaded me from doing an MBA straight after my engineering—was visiting again and I was seated with him and my parents at the dinner table. The man loved India and made it a point to come here every two years. He was probably annoyed that I had not pursued a career in engineering, but he did not mention it. But then, I was even more annoyed that he had pushed me to try a career in engineering in the first place and I did not mention it either. So between us, one could say it was a draw in terms of exhibiting etiquette and good manners.

Now he wanted to know how I was doing in my MBA. It was in response to this that I had just told him about the hunky dory nature of things and my marketing stint at Gronollers.

'That's great,' he said. 'And are you majoring in marketing?' I nodded. 'So which companies are you applying to?'

'Gronollers, Unilever and P&G,' I said. The professor nodded in approval. 'And Citibank, Bank of America and Deutsche Bank,' I continued. The professor stopped nodding and began to stare at me goofily. So I stopped speaking and looked at him enquiringly.

'Those are banks!' he cried.

'Yes,' I said, 'just as their names suggest. I'm also applying to BCG, JNLF and Arthur Anderson. They are consulting firms,' I added.

'But why?!' The professor's voice was raised. I couldn't understand his agitation. Or his question.

'I'm sorry,' I said. 'I don't understand the question.'

'Why... on... earth... are you... applying for... jobs... in banks... and consultancies?' he said, speaking slowly and introducing dramatic pauses within his question. 'You've specialized in marketing and you just finished a summer internship in marketing, which you say you enjoyed.'

Ah, I could now see his confusion. 'Sorry, I should clarify,' I said, 'I am majoring in marketing in that I'm taking more courses in marketing than others. But I'm also doing a few finance courses—to enable me to apply to banks—and a few economics and general business strategy courses that will help me apply for consulting firms.'

'But why?!'

Was he not listening to my answers? It was my turn to speak slowly: 'So that... I can... apply... to banks... and consulting firms.'

'I mean why apply to banks and consulting firms at all? Why not only marketing?'

'Because,' I explained patiently, 'banks and consulting firms come to campus on day 1, which means they are ranked higher. Even the best marketing jobs like the ones I'm applying for are all on day 2.'

I thought he would finally understand this simple, straightforward logic and keep quiet but he did not. He began to browbeat me about the importance of enjoying one's work, finding a passion that one can pursue for life, doing what feels good, working...

Aha! I suddenly realized he was going the same way as he did a few years ago when he talked me out of doing an MBA. And like the last time my parents were listening with rapt attention to his lecture. Now while many people have called me an idiot on many occasions, very few have had a chance to call me an idiot on the same topic twice (I always give them a different topic). In other words, I was prepared this time.

'Yes, I enjoy marketing as I told you,' I said interrupting him in the middle of a rambling story he was relating about Albert Einstein and his love for science that seemed to be going nowhere. 'But I was remiss not to mention that I also love finance as well as economics and general strategy. In fact, I love all my courses in MBA. So all three career options are valid and accordingly I've prepared three distinct resumes—one each for marketing, banking and consultancy.'

He did not pursue the subject, though from the sorrowful way he shook his head I could see he was not entirely convinced.

A heavenly auto ride

As if the problems posed by the IIMA curriculum were not enough, I had now acquired an additional one: how to run into Vidya Thampi again? While this was the most interesting problem in my list (the others being brain-deadening puzzles like *helping the HR manager handle a tricky negotiation with the workers' union at Monolithic Forge* and *optimizing production at Easy-Weasy Textiles during the off-season*), it was also the most difficult.

My mind was preoccupied by Vidya Thampi, and little else. She lived less than a kilometre away but she might as well have lived on the moon, such was the distance between students and staff in the after-college hours. While I could seek the help of my more erudite classmates to tackle the problems of negotiating with workers and optimizing production, who could I consult on this?

Then I thought of Umesh Goregaonkar, the man whose suggestion that I hand in my late POM report to Professor Thampi at his house had led to my meeting Vidya in the first place. Unlike my other mates, he already knew how I met Vidya. So, I invited him for tea at Soma's and laid bare my soul, so to speak.

'Do you understand my complex problem?' I asked anxiously when I had finished.

'Not complex,' he said, 'just surprising. You want to cultivate a romance with the direct descendant of the ogre Thampi?'

'She's not a bit like her father,' I said. 'She's a sweet, pleasant angel. Did I tell you how, when I reached the professor's house, Vidya...'

'Four times,' Goregaonkar said firmly. 'Let me think.' A minute later he continued: 'Why don't you visit the professor at his house to ask him a question on POM?'

'Visit Thampi?' I said. He nodded. 'At his house?' He nodded but with less vigour. 'Without full-body armour protection?'

'Okay, that won't work,' he said and frowned in thought. 'Got it! Ring her up. I'll get you the number from a clerk I know at the office.'

'What if the professor answers?' I said in horror.

'Hang up. But take care to call when he's in the college teaching a class.'

'But what do I say when Vidya comes on the line?'

'I don't know,' he said impatiently. 'You're the one smitten. Think of something. Invite her for coffee or something.'

By the next morning, I decided to try Goregaonkar's idea. He got me the phone number as promised. I approached a campus telephone instrument ('local calls only') and nervously dialled the number. As the phone rang, I started to panic. *What if the professor answered? He was supposed to be teaching a class but what if he had cancelled it at the last minute and gone home? Or what if, like the devil (or was it the werewolf?), he could be in two places at once?* I nearly put down the phone in fear, but a female voice answered, 'Hello?'

'Hello,' I said in relief. 'Is it Professor Thampi's residence?'

'Yes,' she said.

I couldn't be sure if it was Vidya. 'And who is speaking?' I asked.

'I should be asking that question,' she said firmly—it was definitely not Vidya. 'Whom do you want? And who are you?'

'Ganapathi Venkateswariya,' I blurted out, wincing immediately.

'And do you want to speak to Professor Thampi, Mr Venkateswariya?'

'Yes,' I said. 'I'm his student. But it's okay. I'll call later.' I put down the phone in a hurry.

Later, when I related the conversation to Goregaonkar, he did not sympathise with me.

'You should have simply said you wanted to speak to Vidya,' he said. 'Try again.'

'Never! What will I say: "Ma'am, when I said husband, I really meant your daughter"? I can't.'

'I need time to think of another idea,' said Goregaonkar. 'But you're sure to muck that one up too.'

Luckily I didn't have a chance to. The next day was Saturday and our inter-dormitory basketball matches were going on. I dutifully reached the court with my dorm-mates to cheer our team. Soon the game was in full swing.

'*D14 ka tempo high hai! D14 ka tempo high hai!*' we screamed. And whenever our team scored we switched to the more aggressive chant, '*D6 ki le li... Jing Chak! Jing Chak!*' repeatedly. Opposite us, showing no originality, our foes' supporters yelled, '*D6 ka tempo high hai! D6 ka tempo high hai!*' and '*D14 ki le li... Jing Chak! Jing Chak!*'

In the middle of this frenzied chanting I glanced at the spectators standing on the side and, to my surprise, saw Vidya there. She saw me look at her and grinned. I stopped

'Do you all behave like this in class too? I mean, if you answer the professor's question correctly, does the whole class go: "Jags ka tempo high hai! Jags ka tempo high hai!" and "Professor ki le li... Jing Chak! Jing Chak!?"'

shouting and waved to her. When she waved back, I walked over. We stepped a few paces away from the frenzied spectators so that we could hear each other.

'I'm from Dorm 14,' I said, to open the conversation.

'I gathered as much,' she said, smiling. 'But do you all behave like this in class too? I mean, if you answer the professor's question correctly, does the whole class go: '*Jags ka tempo high hai! Jags ka tempo high hai!*' and '*Professor ki le li... Jing Chak! Jing Chak!?*'

'No!' I shook my head. 'Firstly I don't often answer professors' questions correctly, but even if I did...' I suddenly began laughing. 'Can you imagine us doing this in your dad's class?!'

She laughed too. 'Yes, it's a bit hard to imagine. But actually my dad is quite a softie if you get to know him well.'

This was pure nonsense of course, but hearing her come to the defence of the blackguard made me adore her even more. A sweeter seraph I had never met (actually I had not met *any* seraphs, but you know what I mean).

'If you say so,' I said and plunged forth with the Key Question: 'Would you like to join me for coffee somewhere?'

'Now?' she asked. I nodded. 'But D14 is trailing 18-22. Don't you want to provide moral support?'

There is a time to display dorm loyalty and a time to absolutely not.

'No!' I said firmly. 'Let's go.'

We caught an auto rickshaw at the main gate. Vidya, being the well-versed local Ahmedabad resident, instructed the driver where to go, while I sat in a happy trance next to her. She looked lovely in a green salwar kameez. We sat in close proximity, our bodies almost, but not quite, touching. I could detect a faint, lavender-like scent of shampoo from her hair. Fluttering in the breeze in the open vehicle, her duppatta kept touching my face. I did not object.

I learnt she was in her final year of a BA programme in history at the local university. She had come with her classmates to watch the inter-dormitory games as a lark.

'Do you often come to the IIM campus?' I asked.

'No,' she said. *Was she blushing?* 'Actually, I was hoping I might run into you.'

'Me?!' I felt a surge of emotion in my chest that was difficult to describe. When I was 15, I had felt a sense of thrill when I defeated a boy two years older than me in an under-18 tennis tournament. My feelings now were about fifty times stronger. 'What made you think of me after so many days?'

'Not that many,' she said. 'You called home only yesterday.'

Now it was my turn to blush. 'You know about that?' I said sheepishly.

'At dinner last night, my mother told my dad that his student Ganapathi Venkateswariya had called home to speak to him. Dad was shocked that a student actually called his residence to speak to him. It hasn't happened in 30 years of teaching.'

'Especially since he doesn't have a student named Ganapathi Venkateswariya,' I said.

'Oh, dad doesn't remember the names of most of his students,' she said. 'But he's unlikely to forget Ganapathi Venkateswariya, the One Who Dared to Call. I recognized it, of course. And I came to your campus to see if I would bump into you and ask you this. Why did you call?'

'To ask if you'd come with me for a cup of coffee,' I said.

'Well, I'm doing that now,' she said, still smiling.

'Yes, you are,' I said happily.

The MBA man turns to consultancy

I DON'T THINK I EVER ENJOYED coffee as much as I did that day with Vidya—though I can't remember whether I drank coffee or tea. That coffee (or tea) meeting was followed by others at regular intervals, interspersed with meetings over dinner, all blissful affairs. I also visited her home a few times. I felt that even her father, the hard-nosed professor Balakrishnan Thampi, had begun to thaw towards me. He still scowled every time I showed up at his house but he had stopped saying 'You? Again?!' in that disgusted voice. (Vidya's mother was charming and sweet.)

Between these blissful meetings, of course I had to go through numerous not-so-blissful quizzes, examinations and project reports that continued at their usual relentless pace, such that, before I knew it, I was in my last term at IIMA! Two years of toil and perspiration were coming to an end. My classmates and I could see the light at the end of our dark tunnel. We would no longer have to analyse reams of boring reports about a company's performance and write another report about it. (At that time we did not know that this was exactly what we would be doing, at an even more feverish pace, in the corporate world.)

It was time for campus placement. I had prepared three tailored versions of my resume. One was specifically worded for a job in a consulting firm. It highlighted my singular ability to develop and articulate strategy at the drop of a hat and cited the courses I had taken to support this. The second was aimed at the banking industry. In this I emphasised the finance courses I had taken and how they had made me very savvy from a fiscal point of view. The third, focused on getting me a marketing job, elaborated on my many marketing courses and projects; it also glorified my summer internship at Gronollers, painting me as someone who understood brands, routinely tracked market share by SKU and had a firm pulse on the consumer—a future marketer in the making, in short.

The IIMA placement process is based on popularity: the stronger the demand for a company, based on the number of applications it receives, the earlier it is scheduled. Under this system, the marketing companies arrived on day 2. Banks and consultancies came on day 1 because more students wanted banking and consultancy jobs. And because banking and consultancy jobs were ranked higher, obviously I had to apply for them. This was just as obvious to many of my other classmates who, like me, did not intrinsically want banking or consultancy jobs. All of us applying for banking and consultancy boosted the rankings... and more people applied. It was all heady and wonderful.

The activity took place at a brisk pace to accommodate more than 100 students being interviewed by about ten companies. The moment I finished one interview, I would be escorted by a student volunteer to another one. They all became a blur and I focused on trying to stay alert enough to know which company I was interviewing for each time so I could avoid saying, 'I've admired Citibank since I was a child of four and have always wanted to work there' during the Grindlays Bank interview.

At the end of the day, I had a job! JNLF Consultancy had hired me (along with four others) to join their Mumbai office.

I was thrilled and immediately rushed to tell Vidya Thampi.

'I made it to JNLF!' I said and waved the offer letter at her.

'Well done!' she said. 'And tomorrow, you have the marketing interviews.'

'No, actually I don't,' I said. 'Having accepted the job, I'm out of placement process.'

'What? Why did you accept then? I thought you enjoyed your summer internship at Gronollers and would have liked to work there.'

'I did and I would. But JNLF is ranked higher than Gronollers and other marketing companies!'

She didn't see the logic straightaway. Being a mere history under-graduate, she lacked the perspicacity of an MBA student, especially one from IIMA. So I explained everything to her patiently and assured her that I would be happy working in consultancy.

'Well,' she said. 'As long as you're happy, it's fine. But when you call your parents, please tell them only this part—that you've found a job of your liking. Avoid the ranking story.'

I realized that her advice was sound and nodded my assent. My parents also lacked the sophisticated intelligence of an IIMA graduate.

Parents meeting parents

'I WANT TO HAVE A serious discussion,' said my mother. 'So please listen carefully and don't change the topic.'

I was having dinner with my parents and younger sister at home. I had arrived in Chennai that morning after completing my MBA at IIMA. After two years of toil and perspiration, I had a two-month hiatus before many more years of toil and perspiration: I was to join JNLF Consulting in July.

I was ready for my mother's 'serious discussion' which she had been having this with me ever since I had landed my first job at Kasiram Motors. But this time, instead of my usual evasive manoeuvres, I had my own serious news to share. So I did the South Indian equivalent of laying down my fork and spoon: I stopped mashing rice with my fingers and gave her my full attention.

'You need to get married,' she said sternly. 'And this time, I'm not sparing you. I've lined up a few…'

'I found a girl, Amma,' I said, interrupting her.

'Don't change the topic!' she said. 'You do this every time. We'll come back to the girl you found. I want to discuss your marriage first.'

I explained that I had not located someone in the Lost and Found section but had found a girl in connection with my marriage. 'Her name is Vidya Thampi,' I said.

'But that's a Malayalee name!'

'Yes, because she is a Malayalee,' I explained. 'She's the daughter of one of my IIMA professors.'

'But where did you have time to go around choosing girls during your MBA? You said your course kept you busy. All the while you've been saying you're not ready for marriage to us, you've been quietly looking for a suitable bride in Ahmedabad!'

I could understand my mother's umbrage. Having had no role in selecting her own husband—who she met for the first time on the day of her wedding—she had been rather looking forward to the vicarious pleasure of selecting a partner for her children. In those pre-internet days, the traditional Indian way of doing this was to spread the word among family and friends and, simultaneously, place an advertisement in the newspaper ('tall Brahmin IIMA-MBA boy from a good family seeks a suitable bride'). You would sift through the responses to identify potential candidates and immediately ask for the girls' horoscopes and hand it over to the family astrologer for a verdict about whether the horoscopes were 'good' and, more important, whether they 'matched' with your son's horoscope (which you would also send to the girl's parents for them to do the same). Then you would go house-to-house to meet the prospective brides, with the good and matching horoscopes, and her family. Matchmaking was a complex industry that brought lucrative revenue to newspapers, helped astrologers earn a livelihood and, most important, gave parents a purpose.

So I could understand my mother's disappointment. I placated her by explaining that I had not taken over the process from her but that had met Vidya by chance.

'How?' she wanted to know.

'I met her when I had gone to Prof. Thampi's house to ask him for some help on the subject he taught,' I said. I thought it prudent to hide the fact that I had gone there to submit a late report and that Vidya had saved my life—or at least my grade in the subject—by sneaking it into the pile without her father's knowledge. 'And slowly our friendship grew.'

As I expected, my parents soon relented. Once they did, they pushed me aside and grasped the steering wheel of my matrimony firmly in their hands, investing the energy they had stored for finding the bride into executing the marriage. The first thing they wanted to do was to make an STD call to Ahmedabad and speak to Vidya's parents.

'Not a good idea,' I said. 'The professor is a cantankerous man, whose temper can melt ice at a distance of four feet at any time of the day. He is particularly dangerous if disturbed after dinner when he likes to quietly listen to Carnatic music on his cassette player.'

Ignoring my advice—behaving, in fact, as if I had not spoken—they shooed me from the room and locked the door. Half an hour later they came out, all smiled.

'Very decent people,' my father said. 'Everything is arranged with the Thampis. A charming lady and a thorough gentleman!'

'Did you dial the correct number?' I asked.

'Of course,' continued my mother. 'The engagement is in Ahmedabad next week.'

'What's this?!' I said. 'I just finished two years in Ahmedabad. I don't want to go back so soon!'

'You're not,' my mother said.

Apparently the ceremony would take place among the two sets of parents and Vidya herself would play a minor, supporting role. I was not needed at all for my engagement.

By the time my parents—and my younger sister who had joined them for the binge—returned from Ahmedabad a few days later, they seemed to have completely forgotten my presumptive behaviour of selecting my own partner.

'Excellent ceremony,' announced my mother. 'Nice family. And we like Vidya. Here, we have brought back pictures—' she unpacked a large photograph album from her suitcase, '—from the ceremony. That's Vidya there in the green sari. Isn't she pretty? I think you will like her.'

'Yes, I think I will,' I said. 'Thank you, Amma. Good choice.'

Hurtling towards the wedding

WHEN MY MOTHER GETS BEHIND something, she displays the same tenacity and I've-got-this-covered spirit that your average dog displays when handed a juicy bone. For example, whenever she came across an interesting recipe in a magazine, she would try cooking it the same day, even if it meant leaving the house immediately to buy the necessary ingredients. And if the dish did not come out quite as it should have, she would try again the next day… and the next, till she got it right. I once remember being greeting by a bowl of caramel custard for five consecutive days when I returned from school.

She displayed the same gung-ho attitude on her return from Ahmedabad, where she had met—and been impressed by—Vidya and her parents. And this time, she had infected my father with the same enthusiasm.

'Let's not delay things,' my mother said to my father. 'We should plan the wedding for December.'

'Yes!' said my father. 'I've started making a list.'

'Hang on, hang on!' I said. 'What's the hurry? Don't worry—I won't change my mind.'

I laughed. They did not.

'I'm not worried about you,' my mother said dismissively. 'I don't want to give Vidya too much time to think about this.'

I tried to explain that she had already had time to change her mind if she wanted to. I reminded her that I was joining JNLF in a month—my first job after my MBA.

'I'll be very busy,' I said. 'I won't be able to do anything for the wedding.'

'Can you turn up for the event?' my mother asked. 'That's all you need to do.'

I pointed out that I would be staying in bachelor accommodation—arranged by the company—in my first year; that my salary would be modest, that my workload… I stopped because I could see I was not making an impression. I could make out my mother's mind was busy churning out lists of things to do in her mind. As for my father, he had left the room while I was talking. I could hear him calling up wedding caterers in the other room.

The consultant

On my first day at JNLF Consultancy, I met my IIMA buddy Krishna Godbole at the reception. We had both arrived bright and early, eager to launch our careers in consultancy, to help companies to buy other companies, to offer CEOs advice on how to run their organizations and to map out the long-term strategy of a firm in the doldrums. I was already excited about my first project: helping the mayor of New York to radically uplift the city's sewage system. But I was also a bit worried.

'I'm a bit worried,' I told Godbole. 'I forgot that there are more manholes at intersections.'

'What on earth are you talking about?' he asked.

'My interview,' I said. 'I was asked to estimate the number of manholes in New York City. I said we should multiply the number of avenues by their average length, do the same for the streets that run perpendicular, add these up and, assuming one manhole per 100 feet, come up with the total. But I should have allowed for an extra manhole at the intersection of these avenues and streets. I hope they've not submitted the analysis yet.'

'What analysis? To whom?'

I looked around to ensure no one was listening; then leaned closer to him and lowered my voice.

'I think JNLF is working on a hot project for the mayor of New York. That's why it was included in my interview.'

'You mean,' he said, 'JNLF was stumped and wanted your help with the answer.'

'Not necessarily stumped,' I conceded. 'But they probably wanted a fresh pair of eyes to look at the problem.'

'And they chose a rookie from IIMA who barely knows how to tie his tie?' he said. 'Don't be silly. It was a theoretical problem to test your reasoning powers.'

'No!' I said. 'They wouldn't waste my time on a mere theoretical problem. Besides, the consultant looked very grave and earnest when he asked the question.'

'Consultants always look grave and earnest,' said Godbole. 'Even when they're drinking whisky. Why would the New York mayor need JNLF to help him estimate the number of manholes in his city? And if he did, JNLF would handle it from their US office, not Mumbai.'

Perhaps, but I was not convinced. In any case, I had done my homework—I had found out that there were 12 avenues and 150 streets in New York City, estimated their average lengths, applied my formula (including the extra for intersections) and arrived at the ballpark manhole number. In short, I was raring to go on this project.

But it appeared I wouldn't have to for the first few days. Our first week was to be spent in Sydney in an intense orientation programme (affectionately called Sucking Eggs Training or SET in the company). It is an annual ritual: every year fresh hires are sent to an exotic location to learn the fundamentals of consulting, meet senior partners, and imbibe the JNLF culture.

'You will learn how to analyse business problems and present conclusions in a succinct, impactful manner,' said our HR manager.

We were excited at the prospect of the trip to Sydney but we thought we already knew 'how to analyse business problems and present conclusions in a succinct, impactful manner' from our MBA education.

We were wrong. We learnt that we had been using the wrong font for headers ('only use Cambria 36'), unimpressive bullet points for our analysis, and ridiculous colours in our charts. To make matters worse, we had not been using the Take-Away Conclusion Box on every slide.

We were to practise our PowerPoint skills by analysing a dummy business case.

'The slides should tell a beautiful story,' the manager training us said. 'Remember: your effort should be 80 percent on form, 20 percent on content.'

'Is it the same guideline for our real work when we get back?' a fellow trainee asked.

'On average,' said the manager. 'But I went as high as 95 percent form, 5 percent content for a client who had done all the analysis. I only had to express it better. I didn't tell him that of course. Now let's form groups of four and get started.'

The four of us from IIMA naturally quickly formed a team and looked around to assess the competition.

'It's not a competition,' the manager continued. 'Now let's get to work.'

All the groups worked after the session in the evenings. We were forced to take a break to join the partners for drinks and dinner but we continued after this.

'Go to sleep, folks,' the training manager said, entering the conference room at 1 am on the way from the bar to his room. 'There are no grades and this will have no bearing on what you will work on.'

We nodded without looking up and continued. Like Edmund Hillary, who did not climb Everest because he was going to be graded, the IIM graduate attacks a case purely because it is there.

Tying the knot

SIX MONTHS AFTER I JOINED JNLF, Vidya and I got married. In typical Chennai style, the wedding took place in a large marriage hall (*kalyana mandabam*) and all the guests arrived with full enthusiasm at 6.30 am The ceremony started at the crack of dawn, with Vidya and me sitting cross-legged on a stage alongside a solemn priest. Our task was to look interested and absorbed as he chanted Sanskrit hymns at us and, every now and then, to perform some innocuous tasks at his instruction. These included repeating critical stanzas after him; moving a twig from place A to place B; alternatively wearing and removing a finger-ring made of rope-like leaves; getting up to fall at the feet of select elders before sitting down again; and rolling coconuts towards each other.

I am not doing full justice to the ceremony—we did a lot more but it is difficult to remember. The typical South Indian wedding is complicated enough; ours was rendered particularly intricate because my parents wanted to see all the Tamil rituals performed and Vidya's were equally keen that none of the Kerala ones were left out. So they found a priest who was well-versed in both and let him loose on Vidya and me. As a result we did many more things than the average couple from either community. For the most part, we did these things with a few people—our parents and close relatives—on stage with us. The rest of the guests simply sat in the hall and chatted with each other... and ate tiffin (South Indian breakfast)... and chatted... and ate lunch... and chatted. They were served coffee where they sat but had to move—in batches—to the dining hall next door for their meals.

Weddings in Chennai are a big social occasion: an occasion for women to come out in full splendour, wearing silk saris of intricate design and a few kilogrammes of jewellery (men simply tie a *vashti* or dhoti—something like a white bed sheet—around their waists and tag along); an occasion for people to meet other people who they last met three days ago at their niece Shalini's wedding; an occasion to exchange gossip; an occasion to eat; and, having eaten, an occasion to exchange gossip about the food. The last is a sacred tradition in Chennai, which boasts a handful of famous wedding caterers. Guests sit in neat rows and servers bearing rice, sambhar, rasam, and a multitude of vegetarian delicacies walk past them, plonking food on the banana leaves that serve as plates. As they eat, and of course at leisure when they're back in the hall, the guests love to discuss the credentials of the caterer, the overall menu offered, the generosity of portions and speed at which they were served and the quality of specific items compared with the same ones they had been served at other weddings ('This is okay but Ramulu's vatha kozhumbu is something else altogether').

In all this activity, they have little time for the actual wedding or the specific people getting married on the particular occasion. I realized this at the end of my wedding ceremony (after two hours of continuous chanting, the priest had finally, reluctantly, run out of things to say) when Vidya and I finally went for lunch. The previous batch was just getting out of the hall and among the people streaming out, I ran into P.K. Balaji, who had studied with me in engineering college.

'Hi PK!' I was surprised to see Balaji there. He and I were not close at college. In fact, I barely knew him.

'Hi Jags!' He seemed equally surprised to see me. 'Fancy meeting you at this wedding! My dad is an old college friend of the bride's father. What about you: are you from the girl's side or the boy's?'

'Actually I'm the groom,' I said. 'And this is my wife Vidya. We just got married. On the stage over there.'

'Oh!' He made a quick recovery. 'Actually I was just about to come and wish you. The ceremony is over, is it? Anyway hearty congratulations!' He shook my hand, then Vidya's, and continued: 'And many happy returns of this wonderful day!'

The sophisticated shopper

AT THE SAME TIME THAT I was learning the ropes of consultancy, I was also acquiring the skills needed as a new husband.

'What can I get you from Delhi? Ask for anything,' I said to my wife, my voice brimming with romance and enthusiasm. 'Within two hundred rupees,' I added, before she got carried away.

JNLF was sending us to Delhi to meet the partners there (and imbibe some pearls of consultancy wisdom from them). It was the perfect opportunity to display appropriate new-husband behaviour.

Reciprocating with appropriate new-bride behaviour, she demurred, but—displaying normal woman behaviour—not for long. She asked for a sweater to combat the chilly December winds of Mumbai. She went on to describe her requirement in detail. I nodded politely but I didn't take notes. After all I was buying a sweater, not an intercontinental ballistic missile. How difficult could it be?

Walking back to my hotel after my meeting in Delhi's Connaught Place, I passed a hosiery shop in Janpath. 'If it were done when 'tis done, then 'twere well it were done quickly,' I said out loud, quoting Shakespeare as I do often when I talk to myself.

Five minutes later, I walked out of the shop, package in hand and smile on lips: at one hundred and fifty rupees, the sweater had come in under budget.

***

Back in Mumbai I spread the object out on the bed with a flourish.

'My God!' my wife cried, but not in new-bride ecstasy. 'What have you bought?!'

'A sweater,' I said coldly. 'Exactly what you wanted.'

She began digressing. 'Has it ever snowed in Mumbai? Have you ever suffered from frostbite? Do the lakes freeze? Has it…'

I interrupted her. 'I don't see where you're going with this.'

'It's thick—like you. That's where I'm going with this. Which idiot will wear this blanket in Mumbai? It's designed for an Eskimo suffering from cold.'

I picked up a ruler lying on the desk and measured the sweater: it was 4 mm thick.

'Okay,' I said. 'Perhaps it's a bit over-designed for Mumbai's weather. But no problem—you can wear it when we go somewhere cold for a holiday.'

'I will never wear this horrendous flame red colour.'

'You don't like it?' I asked, surprised, 'But the shopkeeper particularly recommended it.'

'I asked for black. And I told you where to buy it. But of course you cleverly realized that what I *really* meant was: "Enter the first undergarment shop you see and follow the recommendation of the fifty-year old male shopkeeper".'

'Don't worry,' I said, valiantly trying to salvage something. 'We can dye it; *then* you can use it when we go on a holiday to a very cold place. We couldn't have done

'At least try it on. Then we can imagine how it will look on you in black... in winter... in Kashmir.'

this if you had wanted a pink sweater: you can only dye something into a *darker* colour. There's nothing darker than black!' I laughed.

Vidya could have laughed at the joke or appreciated her luck for not wanting pink or thanked me for the education in dyeing. Instead she shook her head in disgust. I tried harder.

'At least try it on. Then we can imagine how it will look on you in black... in winter... in Kashmir.'

Reluctantly she pulled the sweater over her neck. Immediately I regretted the suggestion. The garment flowed and flowed, ending at her knees. Each shoulder sagged till the elbow. The sleeves ended a long way after her hands did.

'Perhaps, after dyeing it, you may want to cut it into two or three sweaters?' she said.

I almost suggested that it may fit her in a couple of years but better sense prevailed. Instead I offered to exchange it for a smaller, less thick, black sweater on my next trip to Delhi but she beseeched me not to.

On a subsequent Delhi trip, when I tried to get my money back, the shopkeeper was not amused. With the aid of a magnifying glass kept beside him for this purpose, he showed me the small print behind the bill that stated that they did not refund cash. He allowed me to buy something else in exchange.

I learnt two valuable lessons that day. The first was that a hosiery shop mainly sells undergarments. In fact, apart from two sweaters (one of which I had just returned), this shop sold nothing but briefs, vests, stockings and socks. The second was the price of one sweater covers a lot of underwear and socks. I left the shop with enough undergarments to last me three decades.

Getting the first consultancy project

At last the on-boarding programme at JNLF was complete. We had learnt how to create, modify, beautify, and embellish PowerPoint slides so that our presentations would glow in the dark and sparkle when opened. We had absorbed so much ambrosia of consultancy acumen from senior partners that it was oozing out of our pores. Equipped with the right weapons, we were ready for war.

I walked into the JNLF office keen and eager to consult, to take on projects of tremendous portent and change the trajectory of troubled companies. As I sat down at my desk, I wondered which problem I would be asked to solve.

Unfortunately, I knew it would not be New York's sewage problem. During one of the social dinners I attended as part of the on-boarding programme, I had cornered the manager who had interviewed me at IIMA and asked him if JNLF had been retained by the New York mayor.

'No,' he said, sounding surprised. 'Why do you ask?'

'When you interviewed me on campus, you asked me how many manholes there are in New York.'

'Oh, that?' He laughed. 'Did you seriously think we needed the correct answer to that question? And that we actually would have trusted a mere college student to give us the answer?' I wanted to tell him that it was not appropriate to describe an IIMA graduate as a 'mere college student', but out of politeness (and a certain instinct of self-preservation), I did not. 'That was a question to test your reasoning powers, which judging by your question just now, appear to be shaky.' He guffawed (I did not join him) and clipped me on the shoulder. 'Don't worry—I was kidding. But I remember asking another candidate to estimate the diameter of Saturn. I hope she did not think we have been retained by the mayor of Saturn!' He laughed even louder and thumped me even harder on the shoulder. I had not previously met a man with such a high appreciation of his own sense of humour.

So as I was saying, it appeared that the New York project, such as I had envisaged it, was a non-starter. But surely there would be other equally challenging assignments waiting?

I looked around me. I had been sitting for fifteen minutes and, surprisingly, no manager had come to me with a ripe project ready to be devoured. They must all be in a meeting, I thought, as I noticed my fellow new hires sitting similarly idle, but eager for work, at their desks. Soon the morning passed, the lunch break came and went, and we were still sitting idly. Over afternoon tea, a few of us thought we should make an enquiry. So we trooped into the HR manager's room.

'Yes?' he asked politely.

'We've finished our on-boarding programme,' we said, 'and we're ready to work.'

'Yes,' he said. Then, as he saw us waiting expectantly, added: 'Well done!'

We explained that while we were ready to work, no work had been given to us all morning. We expected him to jump up in surprise at such talent lying waste for a whole morning. Instead he made us jump in surprise with his response.

'You will get assigned to a project when the partner on that project requires some extra grunt help—sorry, I mean, some additional intellectual resource. You have to wait.'

'You mean there are no projects already assigned to us?' He shook his head. 'But during our interview we were told that JNLF was going through a manpower crunch with a large number of projects and plans to expand?'

'That is true,' said the HR stalwart. 'But each partner has profit responsibility and is very careful about adding unnecessary costs to his projects. Don't worry: something will come up for each of you in the next few days.' I breathed a sigh of relief. 'Or weeks.'

I gasped. 'It could take weeks?'

'Or more,' he said. 'It depends on the partner and the project. But don't worry. If you don't get assigned anything, I might offer you cost-free. That way the partner can get extra labour without paying for it. So one way or the other, you'll have work. Meanwhile, enjoy the scenery—' he pointed vaguely around the office lined with scenic cubicles '—read stuff, get acquainted with the company and meet people.'

We had walked into his office feeling like crisp and chirpy 'consultants'. We walked out feeling like damp and wilted 'unnecessary costs'.

The dynamic, supercharged, recently-trained executive

In my first week at JNLF, along with my fellow fresh hires, I attended the intense SET (Sucking Eggs Training) programme. So I was well-versed with the concept of helping rookies learn how to operate in a new company. But, about a year after passing out of IIMA, when I got a phone call from my classmate Pankaj Mehta, I realized that JNLF was merely scratching the surface in this new-hire-training department compared to Washington Weatherbee, the multinational consumer goods company that Mehta had joined.

'I've just been through an amazing Executive Effectiveness programme!' Mehta sounded excited.

'Let me guess,' I said, stifling a yawn. 'It's about how to make your PowerPoint presentations more effective.'

'Of course not!' he said. 'This is a comprehensive programme aimed to develop leadership in young executives.'

'Really? Tell me about it,' I said.

He was happy to do that but felt he could not do justice over a telephone line. So he invited me for lunch the next day at a fancy restaurant. I was impressed. In group outings at college, Mehta was notorious for leaving 'my wallet in the dorm by mistake'. The training programme must include a section on Winning Friends through Generosity, I thought.

I reached the restaurant on time and glanced around. In a mirror on the wall, I could see Mehta lurking in the corridor. Curious, I approached him.

'Oh, you're here?' he said. I nodded because I was.

'In the course,' he said, 'they taught us not to reach very early for an appointment: it shows over-eagerness. So I was waiting for you to arrive first.'

'But I could see you in the corridor,' I said, 'Next time, hide in the toilet; then climb out of the window and approach the restaurant from the main door again.'

He nodded and made a note in an elegant notebook he was carrying. After we ordered our food, he referred to this notebook; then looked earnestly at me and said: 'Tell me about your tennis problems.'

I was surprised. Mehta, whose passion was bridge, had never shown any interest in the game of tennis, leave alone *my* tennis, previously. Pleased at this sudden interest, I spoke eagerly.

'It's the topspin backhand I'm getting nowhere with. I've watched...'

Mehta interrupted me. 'Let's see if I understand you. You say you're not getting anywhere with the topspin backhand?' He was staring deep into my eyes in the most disconcerting manner.

'Yes,' I said, 'I've watched professionals do it a thousand times but...'

'You say you've observed tennis pros hit the same shot a thousand times?'

I nodded. 'But when I try the same thing, the ball flies all over the place.'

'You're saying when you try the same…'

'Why are you repeating everything I'm saying?' I asked.

'I'm practising being Empathetic,' he said, 'by paraphrasing what you say. It's the first step in Listening that we learnt. Please go on.'

I didn't have the heart to tell him he was behaving more like an Annoying Parrot than an Empathetic Listener. The food arrived and, to avoid continuing this painful conversation, I quickly attacked it.

'Stop!' Pankaj screamed. 'You're eating all wrong! We always bring food to mouth with the fork in the right hand in America.'

'We're Indians eating in India,' I reminded him.

'Ah! That's where you're wrong,' he said, shaking his head and wagging his index finger close to my face. 'We're not Indians in India. We're global citizens living in a globally connected world today. Besides, we both work for American corporations, don't we? Let me show you the right way.'

He reduced my lunch enjoyment by 75 percent by providing the following coaching on cutlery usage: cut food with knife in right hand and fork in left; carefully lay down knife; transfer fork from left to right hand; pick up food; put gently into mouth; transfer fork to left hand; pick up knife with right hand… then repeat steps A to G. The topspin backhand is easier than this, I thought.

Suddenly, in the middle of telling me the names of the course instructors, Mehta banged the table hard with his fist, causing me to drop the fork (in my right hand) and spill lasagne all over my trousers.

'What happened?' I asked.

'I'm practising being Emphatic,' he said.

'But you do that by repeating what you hear.'

'No, that's when I'm being Empathetic. Now I'm being Emphatic... or Forceful.' He banged the table harder and shouted, 'WAITER!'

Our waiter hurried over. 'I asked for chives in my gnocchi. Change this!'

As the waiter scurried away with his plate, Pankaj turned to me and winked. 'Just practising. I didn't actually ask for chives.'

During the next half hour he imparted many lessons: what to wear for the second negotiation; how to adapt your persuasion style to suit the gravity of the topic, the mood of your audience and the texture of the carpet in the room; and how to close the sale by asking for the order.

At last we finished our meal. As the waiter brought the bill, Mehta rose from his seat.

'Get this,' he instructed me tersely. 'I forgot to bring my wallet.'

Some traits are beyond training, I thought.

'Let's meet next week,' Mehta continued. 'And let's do Chinese. I can show you how to use chopsticks while simultaneously teaching you how to handle a conflict situation in the winter months.'

The known unknowns

A CONSULTANCY NEEDS CLIENTS TO MAKE money. Therefore a lot of consulting time is spent in acquiring new clients. It fell on the partners—the senior fellows who run the consultancy—to identify new clients and convince them to use our services (so we could charge them for it). Partners were always looking for opportunities to pitch for new business: at their office desks, while attending meetings, while eating lunch, during the drive back home and while tucking their kids into bed for the night.

I remember the days we were preparing to pitch for the business of a food company (called Merry Foods) eyeing the ready-to-bake market. Even during our lunch break, when we were talking idly of this and that, I realized our partner Anup Biswas's mind was still on the briefing session with the client scheduled for the next day.

'Listen to this statement from the former US Secretary of Defence Donald Rumsfeld,' Biswas said, taking out a paper from his pocket. 'I'm quoting: "As we know, there are known knowns. There are things we know we know. We also know there are known unknowns. That is to say we know there are some things we do not know. But there are also unknown unknowns, the ones we don't know we don't know." Is that deep or what?'

'Yes, we don't know the positioning. But we know we don't know. What about what we don't know we know about the market?'

We nodded a little uncertainly. It certainly *sounded* deep but what exactly did it mean?

'Mr Rumsfeld's statement has inspired economists Salvatore Modica and Aldo Rustichini,' continued Biswas. 'They talk about a person being *certain* when he knows something; *uncertain* when he does not know it but he knows he does not; and *unaware* when he does not know it and he does not know he does not know. The psychoanalytic philosopher Slavoj Žižek suggests yet another category: the unknown known, things we don't know we know.'

I mentally grappled with Mr Žižek's category, trying desperately to find things I knew but did not know that I knew. Perhaps, despite never having ventured more than two feet underwater wearing a funny tight suit, I was intrinsically an accomplished scuba diver?

'Known unknowns and unknown knowns are becoming big, ladies and gentleman,' Biswas said. 'Jeffrey Rotter has called his novel *Unknown Known* and song-writer Bryant Kong has used the words in an opera-like song. The question is: how can consultancy exploit this concept too?' Biswas mediated on the problem as he chewed his biriyani.

He appeared to be in a good mood when I met him at office of Merry Foods, our prospective client, the next day.

'We know the market size, growth rate, major players, their products and positioning,' said the company's CEO as he briefed us. 'What we don't know is the right positioning for our product. We want your recommendation—probably a week's worth of work?'

Anup Biswas laughed gently.

'Marketers delve into "known knowns" but ignore "unknown unknowns",' he said.

'I beg your pardon?' said the CEO.

'Market size, players, that kind of stuff… of course we know, because we know we know! And the positioning for our product—we don't know. But we know we don't know. What about what we don't know we know about the market?'

The client looked puzzled. 'I don't know.'

'Precisely!' cried Biswas. 'But wouldn't you want to know? And what about the things you don't know you don't know?'

'I don't know what you're talking about.'

'Exactly! Even *I* don't know what I'm talking about. If I did, we would not *not know* what we don't know. Understand?'

'No.'

'Good! If you did, it would mean you know what you don't know, which is useless. JNLF will help you by analysing secondary data, talking to renowned bakers and doing extensive interviews of consumers. At the end of about 40 days, we'll develop our proprietary *Knowledge Syndrome* of the category, laying out very clearly (a) what we know we know (including what we *definitely* know we know and what we *think* we know we know), (b) what we don't know we know, (c) what we know we don't know and, the most elusive, (d) what we don't know we don't know. Then we'll work two weeks to *enhance* the first category by systematically reducing the other three. Only *then* will we be ready to address your launch plan.'

It was an impressive speech. All of us from JNLF nodded but not as vigorously as the client.

'When can you start?' he said.

A man's monthly syndrome

'IMAGINE THIS IS THE NET,' I said to my wife, carefully placing a knife lengthwise on the table with its sharp side up 'and this area my court.' I placed a table mat on one side of the knife. 'His serve landed in this corner and my backhand slice return…'

'Oh, enough of your stupid tennis!' Vidya snapped and stormed out of the room.

In shock, I dropped the fork I'd picked up to illustrate where my return had crossed my opponent as he raced to the net. For the past few weekends, I had been captivating Vidya with tales of my tennis exploits and hád got used to receiving polite nods at critical junctures, not having my head bitten off.

The next day, she gave me a perfunctory apology: 'Sorry,' she said. 'It's PMS.'

I nodded without really understanding the deep implications of that statement. And the next week, when I described to her how—through a cunning combination of distracting my fellow workers and moving nimbly—I had managed to seize the last pizza slice at my lunch meeting, she actually smiled. So I thought things were back on an even keel and I had nothing to worry about.

But a few days later she flared up again for no reason (something trivial about my breaking a mug she had had from childhood) and I realized that, in order to be prepared for my future with this woman, I needed to brush up my knowledge on PMS.

My initial research told me that, during her premenstrual syndrome, 'a woman's central-nervous-system neurotransmitter interacts with sex hormones and this affects serotonin activity in the brain,' which would have been very helpful if I had had a master's degree in biology. I dug deeper till I found out what I needed to know: the chief symptoms of PMS are unhappiness, tension and, here you go, irritability.

Armed with this knowledge, I learned to tread my way gingerly around my wife on her PMS days, being solicitous and patient and avoiding eye contact. Arguing with a woman is futile at the best of times; when she is PMSing, it's foolhardy. So I would acquiesce on most points, including the necessity of changing channels just as Boris Becker was throwing the ball up to serve for the match.

Things proceeded quite amicably based on this arrangement. As soon as I detected signs of PMS in my wife, I would immediately switch on my courtesy button and become kind and ready to yield to her wishes. However it appeared to me that I was being solicitous and compliant more frequently than the laws of nature would seem to demand. So I began to track my wife's PMS behaviour. After a few months of doing this, I was suddenly horrified to find that the gap between this and her last exhibition of similar irritability was less than two weeks.

'Ha ha!' I said triumphantly, looking up from the diary in which I had made the notation to her. 'You exhibited PMS irritability on the 9th of March. And today is only the 20th of March! You're cheating!'

'What is this?' Vidya asked quietly and, without my permission, took the diary and began going through it. 'Have you actually been tracking my periods?' I nodded. 'How dare you!'

She began giving me a lecture about minding my own business. 'If you had to track something in a diary, why don't you track your exercise routine? I know why—because you don't have an exercise routine!'

'Okay, okay, sorry,' I said soothingly. 'I should not have brought up the topic now in the middle of your PMS.'

'It's not my PMS.' She said it quietly, in a reasonable tone.

'Okay,' I said. I could be reasonable too. 'It doesn't matter. You were just cheating—we all do it sometimes.'

'Are we playing Scrabble?' she asked quietly.

I was surprised, but pleased, at the sudden change of topic. If playing Scrabble would lighten her mood, I was all for it.

'I'll go and bring the board out now,' I said.

'No!' she said, grinding her teeth. 'I meant: do you think we're playing a stupid game here and I'm cheating?'

'No,' I said. 'But according to this diary...'

'Let me have that diary,' she said and, before I could let her, plucked it from my hands. 'Let me make one thing very clear. It's not my PMS. But more importantly: you are not to track it any more. Is that clear?'

I nodded. Though she spoke quietly I could discern—being sensitive by nature—that she was in a nasty mood. So I let her keep the diary and quietly left the room, noting an important lesson in life: a woman is irritable and moody during her PMS—that's a given. But she also reserves the right to be irritable and moody *at any time*.

Difficult conversations

As a consultant, over long conversations with clients, I discovered that their favourite topic is themselves. In my social life I met many people who were *not* clients (thank God!) and their favourite topic was themselves too. Studies have shown that this is true of *all* people, irrespective of their race, country of citizenship and whether they like spicy food or not.

By treating social acquaintances like clients, I developed the art of making small talk: when I met a stranger, I simply got them to talk about themselves. In a few moments we would be deep in conversation.

But the Bell curve (referred to affectionately in mathematical circles as the normal Gaussian continuous probability distribution) applies to people's propensity to talk about themselves too: there are outliers at each end. I met them both at the same party one day.

I was introduced to Prasant Shukla as he sat quietly, sipping orange juice.

'How are you?' I asked to set the ball rolling and leaned back comfortably in the sofa.

'Fine,' he said.

I waited for details about the nature of his well-being or a similar enquiry about my state of affairs. Neither came. After one minute, I began to get fidgety.

'Where do you work?' I asked.

'Bosh!'

'Pardon?' I was taken aback at the rudeness.

'The automotive parts company.'

'Oh, Bosch?' I said, relieved. 'How long have you been with them?'

'Eight years.' He did not elaborate.

'That's a long time!' I said, 'And before that?'

'College.'

The silence began to hang around awkwardly like the string holding my uncle Mahendran's pyjamas.

'So you're off to work tomorrow?' I said brightly.

'No, our factory is closed on Sundays and Mondays.'

He had uttered his first full sentence! Excited, I plunged ahead with a penetrating follow-up question.

'Aha! Then you'll go to work on Tuesday?'

'Yes,' he said.

Perhaps he doesn't like his job, I thought, and made a sharp turn to the left.

'Do you have children?'

'Yes,' he said.

'How many?'

'Two.'

'How old?'

'Nine and seven.'

'Both boys?'

'No.'

'Two girls?'

'No.'

'One of each?!' I yelled triumphantly.

'Yes,' he said.

'And what do they do?'

'School.'

I realized I could have had a better conversation with the wardrobe in the corner. Saying I needed a drink (not a lie), I left him.

Fortified with whisky, I wandered to where my host Hari Menon was sitting with another gentleman.

'Join us, Jags,' Hari said. 'Meet Atul Vasudev.'

'Hi Atul,' I said. 'What do you do?'

'Managing director at Friendly Faucets,' he said. 'My company does not believe in the use of the "CEO" title—' his tone indicated that he, personally, believed in it, '—otherwise you could say CEO at Friendly Faucets. Big company—176 people in the head office itself.'

He told me how he had turned around the company's business in his previous role as sales head through a deft combination of sales-building, cost-cutting and new-client-acquisition, citing two examples of each. The promotion to managing director (or CEO, he clarified) was inevitable. He said it was a tough job but he loved it and explained why… in detail. Soon I knew more about his job than mine, but he had more to tell.

Luckily even managing directors have to breathe. When he did, I jumped in.

'Do you have any children?'

'Yes, two boys,' he said. 'The elder is in his final year in Bombay Scottish, and the younger in class 9. Both are doing very well.' He gave me their academic credentials; then asked: 'Are you wondering if they have any achievements outside their studies?'

I wasn't but he told me anyway. Apparently they had… many.

When he next paused to breathe, I quickly addressed the host.

'How's the golf going, Hari?' Like any avid golfer worth his salt, Hari always had golfing yarns to narrate.

'Great!' said Hari, 'On Sunday, I played in Pune with Ashok and Kailash. On the sixth green...'

'Funny you should mention golf.' Atul Vasudev inserted himself neatly into the conversation. 'I started playing two years ago. I remember telling my wife, "Sheila, we have free company membership. Why not learn golf?" "I could never learn a new game at this age, Atul," she said, "but you go ahead; you play such a wonderful game of badminton, you'll pick it up quickly." In six months, I brought my handicap down to 12.'

Hari had been playing golf for 15 years and had a handicap of 30. I could feel his pain.

'I must tell you the story of my first under-80,' Vasudev continued. 'After bogeys in the first two holes, I approached the third tee...'

'Hang on!' I held up my open palm politely. 'I'm afraid I have to take this call.'

Taking the phone out of my pocket, I trotted away quickly. It was time for whisky again.

Rekindling of an old love

'THE READY-TO-BAKE SEGMENT IS OURS, if we are ready to take it,' said Prashant Ghosh and paused. Satisfied with our murmurs of approval at his clever use of words, he went on: 'Here is a picture of our prospective consumer.'

JNLF had won the Merry Foods consultancy assignment when our partner Anup Biswas made an impressive pitch promising to look into the unknown knowns and known unknowns. In the past two months we had done that work and recommended that Merry Foods go ahead and enter this lucrative market. We were now at a meeting to discuss the upcoming launch of Merry Food's Kwik Bake range of ready-to-bake products with the Merry Foods team, led by their CEO, and a small contingent from Merry Foods' advertising agency, Q&P Advertising. Given the importance of the meeting, Q&P's CEO Prashant Ghost was leading the presentation himself.

Ghosh, a portly man dressed in a smart pinstripe suit, was an advertising veteran and a seasoned orator. As I listened to him converting the complex charts and graphs from JNLF into a colourful marketing story, I was impressed.

'Meet Ms Shobha Malhotra,' he said and flashed the picture of a harassed-looking woman in her thirties standing in her kitchen dressed in a housecoat and holding a saucepan, her hair in disarray and flour marks on her face. She looked like she was about to burst into tears. 'It's 7.30 am and Ms Malhotra, a working woman with two boys aged six and eight, has an important meeting at 10. But it's her younger son's birthday today and, in a burst of enthusiasm, she had promised to bake his birthday cake herself.'

He gave us time to appreciate Ms Malhotra's dire situation; then went on.

'Now Ms Malhotra is a capable human resources manager at work but she is not a capable baker. But she has promised her boy—her dear, six-year old son—a fresh birthday cake baked with her own hands. So she is here in her kitchen, throwing ingredients from her recipe book together and desperately hoping the cake will turn out well. She is also hoping she will reach her meeting—about her company's annual recruitment plan—on time. If the cake turns out poorly, what will her son think of her?'

Ghosh looked around the room sorrowfully. I was moved by Ms Malhotra's plight and I could see my fellow JNLF colleagues nodding sadly too. And as for the Merry Foods CEO, he was wiping the tears from his eyes with a handkerchief.

'Does Ms Malhotra have to go through this agony?' Ghosh continued. 'No! Definitely not! With Kwik Bake, she can bake the most delicious cake in 20 minutes flat.' He flashed another picture on the screen. The same Ms Malhotra, now dressed in a fashionable sari, was smiling into the camera, holding up a plate with a beautiful cake on it. Her hair was tied in a neat plait, her make-up was impeccable and she looked ready to step out and face the world. 'Kwik Bake will transform Ms Malhotra from an expert human resources manager to an expert baker who is *also* an expert human resources manager. That is our mission, ladies and gentleman.'

We clapped. Ghosh went on to quote statistics (from our report) on urbanization and the rise of the working woman and, correspondingly, in ready-to-cook products to ease her life. He then announced that his creative director would now explain the advertising they were recommending.

As the meeting began I had noticed a bearded man in jeans, a t-shirt and sandals sitting in one corner of the room, chewing gum and apparently absorbed in something written in his notebook. I had assumed he was a close relative of Merry Foods' CEO and was therefore allowed to walk, in his unkempt state, into any meeting he liked and potter around uninterested. But now, as this man stood up, I realized he was the creative director.

'Here's the scene. Ms Malhotra is in her kitchen. The door is closed. She is working on her laptop; in the background we see the oven is on. There's a knock on the door. "Is the cake ready, Mommy?" cries her small son from the other side. "No," replies the woman, not looking up from her screen. "And don't disturb me—it's very difficult to bake a cake—you don't want me to mess it up". "Sorry!" cries the little boy. A few seconds later, the oven goes ping, the woman smiles, closes her laptop, deliberately applies some flour on her cheek, messes up her hair, removes the cake from the oven and opens the door to invite her family in. As the family admires the cake and enjoys its fresh, home-made deliciousness, we dissolve to a pack-shot of the Kwik Bake product and the slogan: "Kwik Bake. Make baking a cake-walk". That's it. The print campaign will feature a picture of the woman sitting in her kitchen with her laptop in front of her and the oven on the side. The copy will talk about how easy it is to bake with Kwik Bake ready-to-bake cake mixes. And of course, the same slogan, "Kwik Bake. Make baking a cake-walk", will appear at the bottom.'

He stopped and looked around the room for reactions. We all turned to the Merry Foods chief. 'I love it!' he cried. Immediately, everyone cheered. Then a voice spoke up. It was his marketing manager.

'I like it too. But,' he said a little diffidently, 'the advertisement is to be in Hindi, not English. What is the Hindi slogan?'

'Oh, our translator will take care of it; don't worry,' said the creative director dismissively.

The marketing manager began to say that he felt that a Hindi translation of 'cake-walk', something like *meethi roti paidal raasta,* was neither catchy nor understandable, but the CEO interrupted him. 'The agency will figure it out. Let's move on.'

As the meeting progressed, I felt a rekindling of my old love for marketing and advertising. I was particularly impressed with Q&P and its chief Prashant Ghosh. Later that week, I called him up and talked to him about my background, including my happy experience interning with Gronollers. He invited me for a meeting over a cup of coffee.

The meeting went well and ended with a nice proposal from Ghosh.

'We'd be happy to have someone in our agency with an MBA from IIMA in marketing and a few years of consultancy under his belt,' Ghosh said. 'I'd start you as an account director on a solid account.' He then gave me an indication of the salary (excitingly higher than mine then). 'We can talk about all that some more—think about it first and let me know in a week if you want to proceed.'

The decisive, purposeful executive

BEFORE MAKING A DECISION OF significance, the robust manager—especially if, like me, he has an MBA under his belt—knows that he has to gather data, evaluate the alternatives, weigh the pros and cons of each and then, with clarity and firmness, take the plunge.

Accordingly the very next day after my interesting conversation with Prashant Ghosh, I proceeded to follow this technique. I first called up an IIM classmate who had joined advertising after his MBA.

'Two questions for you,' I said. 'First: how many years does it take for someone joining an ad agency after college to become an account director? And second: do people leave consultancy to join an advertising agency?'

I explained the career choice ahead of me and he gave me his perspective. He also put me on to a couple of other people in his agency. By the end of the day I was armed with all the information I needed and was ready to make my momentous managerial decision after one last step: running it by my wife. She already knew about the offer and was waiting to talk about it.

'The move is definitely a jump,' I said. 'My IIMA classmate Digvijay Sharan who joined advertising told me that it normally took about six to eight years for a fresh graduate or MBA to rise to account director. People joining from marketing companies make it a little earlier. So it looks like I'd be trimming one to three years on the typical career curve to this level. Wow, right?'

Vidya did not go, 'Wow!' In fact she looked sceptical; so I continued: 'I also spoke to a planner in Sharan's company who joined them from Arthur Anderson. She got a jump straightaway.'

'Jags, why did you talk to all these people?' Vidya wanted to know.

Ah! I realized I had to explain the managerial decision making process to her. It was not her fault she did not understand me straightaway: after all, she had not done an MBA.

'Making decisions is a process,' I said, 'that requires one to start at ground zero, which is data collection. To do this, one...'

'What do you want to do?' she interrupted me.

'What do you mean?' I asked.

'Which job would you like to do?'

'That's what I'm trying to find out!' I said. 'By comparing how much time it typically takes and whether I'll be ahead of the curve and...'

'Will you enjoy the job in advertising?' She interrupted me again.

'Definitely!' I said. 'I think so,' I added a few seconds later. Then I reflected on the meeting I had attended with my JNLF colleagues for the Merry Foods campaign with the Q&P ad agency, the meeting that had triggered this opportunity and continued: 'I certainly hope so. I think I have a flair for it.'

'You're sure?'

I nodded.

'Then go for it,' she said.

I was relieved to see that she was seeing things my way. Then I noticed she was smiling.

'What's so funny?' I asked.

'I was thinking that one day, while you're enjoying your marketing job, a banker may come along and offer you a position that you may estimate—in your inimitable MBA way—to be higher than what you might have reached if you had started your career in banking. And you may accept it!'

Though she explained it, I still could not understand what she found funny. But I didn't pursue the point.

The next week I met Ghosh and following that meeting, a few others in his agency. And the end of all the discussion, I quit JNLF and joined Q&P Advertising a couple of months later.

A productive railway journey

AFTER I LEFT JNLF CONSULTANCY I had four weeks of free time before I had to join Q&P Advertising. A perfect time to go somewhere on a holiday, I thought, and consulted Vidya. She agreed and suggested we go to Kochi, her home town in Kerala. So I booked train tickets and in a few days, we boarded the train.

Indian Railways' sleeper class is designed to facilitate brotherhood and eliminate all semblance of personal space, with three people seated on a narrow berth and three others facing them with knees touching. In this close proximity, you can feel your neighbour's breath on your neck as he reads your newspaper over your shoulder.

The first few minutes were spent stowing large trunks of luggage underneath the berths and ensuring the safety of the important ones by securing them to the railing with a chain and padlock; unpacking pillows and mattresses and spreading them on the upper berth; and making sure that the elaborately packed meals—complete with plates, pickle and pappad—were easily accessible.

Once everyone was settled into their seats, the thin, bearded man seated opposite us spoke.

'Are you both married?'

On hearing him, the others in our compartment—a bald man with large spectacles and a couple in their fifties—tuned in.

'Yes,' I replied.

'To each other, yes?' He guffawed and looked around. Everyone appreciated the joke: the compartment rocked with laughter. I smiled and nodded.

'Where did you get married?'

'In Chennai,' I said.

He wanted to know which marriage hall. I told him. He complained that he hadn't heard of it, but luckily the bald man had, and was able to provide a succinct account of where it was, how many people it could accommodate, who owned it and how much it cost to host a wedding there.

The couple now joined the merry inquisition.

'Was it a love marriage or an arranged one?' the lady asked my wife.

'Love,' Vidya murmured.

'That's great!' she said. 'Isn't it?' She looked at her husband to initiate a smooth baton transfer.

'Of course!' The good man took the cue in his stride. 'It's fantastic! Love is great, I always say. One of my classmates from Guindy Engineering College also had a love marriage. He is divorced now.' He gave us a few seconds to digest this; then went on: 'When did you get married?'

'Four years ago,' I said.

'Four years?!' said his wife. 'Where are your children?' She looked around as if expecting them to suddenly materialize. When they didn't, she asked in the accusing tone of a defence lawyer interrogating the state's witness: 'Don't you have any children?'

'No,' said Vidya.

'Ooh!' She sucked in her breath noisily. 'How come?'

We stared back at her, unable to utter a word. Her husband felt he had to explain the question better.

'Is there a problem? Have you seen a doctor?'

We shook our heads.

The bald gentleman now entered the fray with a curt announcement:

'Dr Vaibhav Bhattacharya is the best doctor in Mumbai for sex-related problems.'

This was received enthusiastically by the bearded man. By a remarkable coincidence, his neighbour's niece was married to Dr Bhattacharya's brother-in-law. He said he would be happy to get us an appointment.

Construing our silence as diffidence, the lady said, 'Don't be shy. My niece and her husband did not have children for years. Dr Bhattacharya took one look at her, recommended in vitro fertilization and she got pregnant.'

'The boy is four years old now,' her husband said proudly. 'And is learning to ride a bicycle... gap without the training wheels. They're travelling with us in the next cubicle. Say,' he added anxiously, 'I hope you're okay with in vitro fertilization?'

In a cold voice, I explained that we didn't have children because we didn't want to... yet.

The wife shook her finger at Vidya and said: 'Don't delay having children: women have problems with late childbirth. How old are you?'

'Twenty-six,' Vidya murmured.

'Twenty-six?! That's *very* old... We cannot waste another minute—you need to talk to my niece right now. Archana, come here!' she bellowed.

We were joined by a well-built lady exuding confidence, her husband and the four-year-old bicycling wizard. As we all moved to accommodate them, I looked at my watch: only an hour had passed... During the next sixteen hours, my wife and I acquired considerable knowledge about pregnancy and childbirth.

A year later we had our first child. I believe that train journey was the catalyst.

A rollercoaster bus ride

Now that we were in Kerala for a holiday, the first (exciting) item on the agenda was to visit Vidya's relatives: from the list she gave me, it appeared that she had one in every street.

'So,' I asked Vidya's cousin and our host Unnikrishnan, 'where can we get an autorikshaw?'

'Take the bus,' he said. 'It's cheaper and, in Kochi, also faster. Several years ago, the government here opened up bus transportation to the private sector and many private companies—with endearing names like Ammukutty & Sons, Matthew Brothers and Palliakkachall Travels—enthusiastically entered the fray. Good-old private sector competition ensures the buses run often... and fast.'

As Vidya and I boarded the bus, we observed that, before the private companies could maximize profit in a land seeped in Karl Marx's philosophy, they had to first maximize employment. The Mumbai bus employs one driver and one conductor. I was told by a friend living in Singapore that buses there have just the driver ('And I get the feeling,' he said, 'that the ever-efficient government is looking for a way to eliminate him too'). But the Kochi bus we entered employed five people. Two conductors issued tickets from the front and the back, met at the centre after issuing three tickets each and took a break. The bus had two doors that flapped outwards dangerously and were held in place by two employees called *Killis* (parrots). Parrots rarely open and close doors: the reason for the name was that the *Killi's* job was to shout the name of the destination repeatedly (like a parrot) and entice people to get into the bus. In addition, the bus had one driver. (They would have had two if they could fit in a second steering wheel.)

These five employees worked energetically to fill the bus with passengers. The driver's job appeared to be to drive as fast as possible. He started off with a sudden jerk and thundered down the road with his emergency-siren horns shrieking. Then he spotted a competitor ahead of him and *really* got going. As he tried to overtake, the competitor sped up to prevent him. A Hamilton-Alonso battle took place on the narrow road.

Our bus won the battle and got to the next stop first. Before we stopped, the *Killis* swung outside along with the door, screaming the destination, 'Thopumpady! Thopumpady! Thopumpady!' They heralded waiting passengers in quickly and, since the competitor was close behind, urged the driver to take off quickly again.

However, at the next stop, there was no bus following; so our bus lingered. The driver switched off the engine. The conductors, having ticketed the passengers who had joined us at the last stop, chatted with passengers, who relaxed their vice-like hold of the handrails. A soporific mood descended on the bus, marred slightly by the strident 'Thopumpady! Thopumpady! Thopumpady!' going on outside. Then the spell was broken. The *Killis* spotted the next bus and screamed. The driver took off, tyres screeching. Once again I was thrown up, down and sideways.

The bus did not lack employees but it lacked windows. This allowed the wind to blow furiously through the interior. I could see Kerala women sitting in the front cunningly taking advantage of this by saving on the expense of a hair dryer. Having applied coconut oil to their hair generously and washed it off, they now set it free to enjoy a free blow dry (and allowing the people behind them to enjoy a free coconut-oil-flavoured face wash).

That's when I noticed that the front of the bus had seats reserved for women. Apparently men were required to vacate these seats when a woman needed it. But two men were plonked comfortably side by side on two such seats. They were studiously admiring the scenery through the window and avoiding eye contact with the women standing in the aisle beside them. The strategy was working: Kerala women appeared too shy to actually *ask* a man to get up.

But I knew my wife was made of tougher material. I gestured to her and pointed to the sign above the men. When she saw this, Vidya nodded her thanks to me and quickly tapped the nearest man on his shoulder.

'Excuse me.' Her strong voice carried easily through the bus. 'These two seats are reserved for ladies. Perhaps,' she continued loudly to me, seated at the back, 'they can't read.'

The men scampered to the back of the bus and a grateful college girl joined Vidya on the seat.

The unique work ethic of Kerala

In our first two days in Kerala, we visited fourteen relatives of Vidya (I kept count of the cups of tea I consumed at the rate of one cup per relative). Like our companions on the recent train journey, all of them grilled us with penetrating personal questions about our married life.

'No relatives today,' declared my wife on the morning of the third day, 'I might get violent if I encounter another aunt who would like to know about my mother-in-law's opinion of my cooking. Today we go shopping.'

'No you don't,' said Unnikrishnan, Vidya's cousin and our good-natured host. 'It's a Kerala-wide *bandh*, called by the Communist Party of India (M), one of several we have each year.'

'What happens on a *bandh* day?' I asked.

'Nothing,' he said. 'Everything is shut. No one goes to work.'

'But surely then,' my wife pointed out, 'everyone has time to shop; so the shops can do booming business by staying open!'

'In Kerala, when we say "nothing", we mean it,' her cousin said. 'The shops are the first to down their shutters; even cinema theatres stop playing movies.'

'My God!' said Vidya. 'Well, we might as well visit some more relatives today and finish that job so we can shop tomorrow.'

'And how will you visit them?' asked Unnikrishnan sweetly. 'Buses don't run on a Kerala *bandh*, autorickshaws don't ply and trains don't move. If they could, the CPI(M) would inculcate the *bandh* spirit among Kerala birds and get them to stop chirping.'

'But what if I fall sick on a *bandh* day?'

Unnikrishnan murmured something about this not being recommended, but it was a moot point. Pretending to be sick might get us, with a great deal of dubious explanations, to the hospital, not the residence of Vidya's Aunt Ammukutty.

'Why has the CPI(M) called the *bandh* today?' I asked.

'Because it's too hot.'

'They blame the Congress government for that?!' I cried.

'No, they're protesting against the electricity cuts imposed on a perspiring population by the government. Incidentally these electricity cuts were introduced by the CPI(M) when it was in power a few years ago.'

The next day dawned bright and *bandh*-free. I accompanied Vidya on a small shopping trip to buy an umbrella for Unnikrishnan's mother to replace the one at home, a relic purchased in the 1960s that the good aunt insisted was still 'as good as new'. We alighted from the bus and entered a small shop that sold umbrellas, bed sheets and other paraphernalia of household interest.

'Do you have umbrellas?' Vidya asked the shopkeeper, who was sitting alone on a stool behind the counter. He nodded listlessly.

We waited. He did not move. He was not talking on the phone or busy with other customers: the shop was empty. He was simply sitting.

'Where are the umbrellas?' my wife asked, after waiting fruitlessly for a minute.

'There.' He pointed vaguely towards a shelf inside his shop.

Vidya and I walked to the shelf. There we found two umbrellas, one yellow with white flowers; the other red with the same white flowers. She grimaced at the sight and walked back to the shopkeeper.

'There are just two here,' she said. 'Don't you have any more?'

The shopkeeper looked at us irritably. 'Yes, I have,' he snapped. 'Look properly.' He pointed inside his shop again. This time I noticed that his hand was angled upwards.

'There, look!' I pointed to the back of the shop. Hanging from the roof, there were dozens of umbrellas of different colours and sizes.

'Ah! Much better,' said Vidya. 'Some of them actually don't look horrendous.'

We came back and addressed the shopkeeper, who was still sitting in the same place, showing more interest in the passing traffic than his two customers.

'Can you bring down the umbrellas from up there?' Vidya said,

'Which one?' he asked, getting up reluctantly and reaching for a pole with a hook attached to it.

'All of them,' my wife said.

'Are you going to buy them all?' he wanted to know.

'Of course not!'

'Then why should I bring them all down? And then put them all up again?' I could see his point. This would take a full five minutes and he would miss watching at least four buses and six autorickshaws—not to mention dozens of pedestrians—crossing his shop on the street. 'You select the one you want and I'll bring it down for you.'

'I now know why Aunty is still sticking to her 40-year old umbrella,' Vidya said in disgust as we walked out of the shop empty handed.

A banana or two a day

THE RECEPTION AREA OF THE Q&P office in Mumbai was tastefully done. At one end there was a luxurious sofa set and a coffee table with magazines on it for waiting visitors. The reception counter was sleek and the smiling woman behind it added to the overall sophistication of the office. Soft music played discreetly in the background. But I did not notice these things at first because my vision and mind were completely occupied by a large bunch of bananas that were suspended from the roof and were hovering in front of the reception desk at about face level. It was a jarring sight that diluted the impact of the otherwise elegantly furnished lobby.

I made my way around the bananas and approached the woman behind the counter.

'Jags Srinivasan?' she said as I approached. 'Welcome to Q&P!'

'Thanks!' I said, impressed that she had been expecting me. 'Did you put up the bananas to welcome me too?'

'No!' she cried; then lowered her voice: 'I'd have thought of something more graceful. The bananas are not for you—they're for everyone who enters Q&P. Go on, help yourself. The office peon is under strict instruction to constantly replenish them, four times a day if necessary. You see,' she continued, perhaps noticing the look of bewilderment on my face, 'our CEO Prashant Ghosh is from Leo Burnett, where they have a plate of apples at the reception in every office. He says bananas are better than apples. Frankly—' she lowered her voice again '—I think it's because they're cheaper.'

'Anyway,' she continued, 'Follow me. Mr Ghosh is waiting to meet you. Here take this.' She came around the desk, plucked a banana from the bunch and thrust it into my hand. 'Trust me. It'll help you make a good first impression.'

Feeling a little foolish carrying a large banana in one hand and my bag in the other, I followed her into the office, a large hallway with desks and computers—but very few humans at this time. We went past a few desks and entered an office on the side, which featured a cluttered desk, a couple of chairs for visitors and—you guessed it—a bunch of bananas suspended from the roof.

Somehow Prashant Ghosh looked bulkier seated in his office than he had when I met him at the Merry Foods presentation. He not only filled the large swivel chair behind the desk, but overflowed from it on the sides. In the period since our last meeting, he had acquired a distinguished grey beard that gave him the appearance of a learned doctor. He rose (painfully) when I entered and extended a hand. I quickly transferred the banana to my left hand and shook hands with my right.

'Ah! Having one of our bananas, are you?' he said happily. 'Go on. I'll join you.' He broke off a banana from his bunch and, as he began to peel it, looked at me enquiringly. Reluctantly—I had just had a heavy breakfast and was not in banana mood—I followed his example.

'Here take this. Trust me. It'll help you make a good first impression.'

'An apple a day may keep the doctor away,' he said between mouthfuls, 'but a banana gives you energy. That's why athletes eat bananas during the completion. And energy is what we need in the agency business.' He thumped his table enthusiastically as he said that. 'Besides,' he continued, 'we don't want to necessarily keep the doctor away. He is our client!'

He guffawed loudly and looked at me in the identical why-are-you-not-following-me way he had looked a few seconds earlier. I quickly took the hint and laughed politely.

'Yes sir,' he said, squeezing a bit more juice out of the joke, 'Q&P does a lot of pharmaceutical advertising—we definitely don't want to keep the doctor away! I think Leo Burnett went after the wrong fruit.'

According to what I had read, Leo Burnett's penchant for welcoming people with apples had had nothing to do with his belief in their health-providing or keeping-doctor-away benefits. The story was that he had opened his agency during the Great Depression of the 1930s and a Chicago newspaper columnist had predicted that he would fail so miserably that we would soon be on the street selling apples instead. Upon reading those words, Leo had vowed to give away apples instead.

But there was no need to point this out to Ghosh now, I thought.

An angel joins the family

When our first child was born, approximately a year after that fateful railway journey, we were thrilled. The girl, who we named Preeti, was pretty as a picture—and we took dozens of pictures to prove it—as well as intelligent and active at the same time.

One day, about two months after her birth, when Preeti had retired for an early evening nap and Vidya and I were relaxing by going through one of her (Preeti's, not Vidya's) photograph albums, my old IIMA friend Umesh Goregaonkar, walked into our house, the door being open.

'Hello, hello, hello,' he shouted. 'How are the love birds doing?' Goregaonkar was the man I had consulted when courting Vidya.

'Shhh,' I hissed at him, while Vidya hurriedly left the room to check whether Preeti, who was sensitive in addition to being intelligent and beautiful, had been woken up by the uncouth bellowing.

'How's the baby?' he whispered, taking the seat on the sofa next to me that Vidya had just vacated.

'Beautiful,' I assured him. 'Here, take a look.' I put the album on his lap and opened it to the first page. Meanwhile Vidya returned, gave me the thumbs-up to indicate baby-not-woken-by-loud-rascal and took the seat on the other side of Goregaonkar.

'Really beautiful,' said Vidya, neatly taking over, 'She was 8.5 pounds at birth. 8.5 pounds! Can you imagine it?' It looked like Goregaonkar could, quite easily, because he did not show astonishment. 'And she had hair on her head! Black hair! We were amazed.'

As Goregaonkar took this incredible news also in his stride, I provided him some additional perspective. 'The doctor said that Preeti was one of the most developed babies he had ever delivered.'

At last, the man was impressed. 'That's fantastic,' he said, shaking his head in wonder.

We agreed with him and between us, described our daughter to him in detail. I let Vidya go first but when I found her missing out some critical information—how Preeti's eyes twinkled when we rang a bell even if she couldn't see it, for example—I took over, only to allow Vidya to come back when she had something to add. In this way, exhibiting coordinated team behaviour, we went through two photograph albums and had just started on the third when Preeti interrupted us with a long wail of anguish.

Obviously Vidya and I immediately rushed from the room, already cooing on the way. It was baby's feeding time, so I left Vidya to it and returned to the living room. I thought I would find Goregaonkar immersed in album number 3 but for some reason, he had picked up a magazine and seemed very engrossed in it.

I plucked the magazine neatly from his fingers and gazed earnestly into his eyes.

'She's extremely intelligent, as you just saw,' I said. 'Whenever she's hungry, sleepy, lonely or simply uncomfortable, she cries at once. Very sharp mind for a two-month old.' I elaborated with specific examples of

Preeti's intelligence. And, though he glanced at his watch a couple of times—he probably had another appointment on his mind—I could see Goregaonkar was mesmerised by the way he listened.

While I was talking, Vidya returned and announced: 'You may see the baby now.'

'I've not yet finished.' I turned to address her coldly but when I turned back, Goregaonkar wasn't there. He had leapt from the seat and was already halfway to the bedroom. So Vidya and I followed. We stood to one side so he could better admire the baby lying on the bed. After giving him a few minutes, we made our way to the other side.

'Whom does she resemble?' I asked as we posed together so he could make the comparison.

'Both of you.' He said it so quickly, I was not sure he had examined us properly, so I asked for specific details.

'Her nose is Jags',' he said, 'but eyes are Vidya's. Definitely. Forehead is also Vidya's but chin is Jags'.'

This was different from what my parents—who had just returned to Chennai after visiting us—had said and I pointed this out but he stuck to his guns.

'You asked for my opinion and I gave it to you.' He sounded hurt.

'Jags didn't mean you're wrong,' said Vidya soothingly and gave me a glare. 'Your opinion is important. Let's look at the third album in more detail to see how her forehead is like mine and chin like Jags'. We have some group photographs of the three of us together—we can better make the comparison on those.'

She led him back to the drawing room. When I followed a few minutes later, they were just turning the last page of the album.

'Wow!' said Goregaonkar, heaving a sigh of contentment. 'That was terrific.'

'You haven't seen the best yet,' I said, sitting down and placing album number four on his lap. 'These were developed just yesterday and capture my parents' visit.'

I showed him completely different—and captivating—pictures of Vidya with my mother, with my father, with both, and a few with all of us along with the neighbour's dog (a poodle).

Goregaonkar leaned back with another deep sigh when I finished. 'Luckily, I mean unluckily, you don't have a handycam,' he said.

'That's where you're wrong!' I cried, shaking a finger at his face and laughing. 'While Vidya was showing you album number 3, I fixed the VCR and TV set in the other room. Come!'

We took him through an intriguing and dynamic perspective of the child because movements and voices allowed her character to come through in a very different way. Goregaonkar watched silently, too moved to speak.

'Join us for dinner,' Vidya said when the 45-minute video had run its course. 'It's just some simple *pulao* and *raita*.'

'Sure!' he said, perking up. 'I love *pulao* and *raita*!'

Soon we were seated at the table with the two simple dishes in front of us. As Goregaonkar reached for the *pulao*, I remembered something.

'By the way, Vidya, did the baby do potty today?'

'Oh, yes!' she exclaimed. 'I completely forgot to tell you. She had a very good motion.'

'Ahem!' Goregaonkar coughed politely. 'Can we eat now?'

'Of course!' said Vidya. 'Don't be formal, Umesh. Please start.'

'That's great!' I said, continuing where I had left off. 'What time did she do potty?'

'4.35 pm,' said Vidya. 'No, I'm lying. At 4.35 she began straining. Actual potty began more like at 4.38.'

'Straining for three minutes?' I was concerned. 'Was it very hard?'

Vidya assured me that, on the contrary, it was quite soft.

'And was the texture smooth?'

'Yes.'

'What was the colour?' It was then that I noticed that Goregaonkar was still holding the serving spoon poised in the air. His plate was empty. 'Go ahead, Umesh,' I said. 'Serve yourself. Vidya and I will follow.'

But the poor fellow had got a sudden stomach ache and just couldn't eat. In fact, he said he would have to leave now.

'But I thought we'd chat after dinner,' I said. 'I wanted to show you Preeti's toys.'

'No, no, I really have to go now,' he said, walking to the door. 'I'll let myself out. You guys carry on.'

'Poor fellow's stomach must be really hurting,' I said, reaching for the *pulao*. 'Anyway, please continue: you were telling me about the colour of the potty.'

Driving the angel to sleep

I MAY HAVE MENTIONED THIS BEFORE but it's worth repeating. Our daughter Preeti was a beautiful baby, who was also, remarkably, very intelligent, sensitive and active. Some people could not discern these qualities easily at first glance, so we had to enlighten them patiently till they got it.

But our doctor P.M. Samant, an elderly Maharashtrian with grey hair and a stern manner, seemed blind to our daughter's charms and, though we had carried a small portable photo album with us to explain things on our first visit, he showed no interest in going through her photographs.

That visit was prompted by our deep anxiety at Preeti's uncontrollable bawling through much of the previous night.

'The baby is too big,' Dr Samant declared, shaking his head seriously. 'She's overweight.'

We were shocked. It was the first time we had heard anything so blasphemous.

'No, Doctor!' I protested.

'Yes,' he said emphatically. 'Decidedly overweight.'

'Doctor,' I said keeping my temper in check. 'It's her bones that are big.'

'Maybe. But even accounting for that, she's overweight.'

'No Doctor!' Without realizing it, I had raised my voice. But how else to get through to this obtuse man? I tried to speak in a calmer tone: 'It's her bones. Look at me.'

I stood up so he could appreciate the big bones my daughter had—through no fault of her own—inherited.

'Exactly,' the doctor said, looking at me up and down. 'That's what I mean. You're feeding her too much! Cut down her food.'

He then went on to explain that her ailment was nothing more than harmless colic pain that some gripe water—and, he emphasised again, a leaner diet—would easily fix.

When we left the Dr Samant's clinic, I was in an irritated mood. My wife, judging by her frown, appeared equally put off. And as for our daughter, she was howling in pain. Since she had just had a large spoon of gripe water, I was convinced that the tears were caused by the doctor's harsh words (didn't I mention that Preeti was uncommonly intelligent for an infant?).

Such was my level of distraction that I heralded Vidya into a taxi instead of its cheaper cousin, the autorickshaw, many of which were available nearby.

We had travelled perhaps half a kilometre when Preeti stopped crying. She lay in my lap, looking serene and relaxed; her head was tilted back and a small smile lit up her face. Then the taxi stopped at a signal. Immediately Preeti started howling again, stopping only when the signal turned green and the taxi moved forward.

'Wow!' I said. 'The girl can actually recognize the traffic signal already. Amazing!'

'I think it's the motion of the car she loves,' said Vidya. 'See—she's nodding off.'

It was true. My daughter had slipped into sleep. And she continued to sleep as we reached home, carried her inside and tucked her into her bed. Vidya and I looked at each other in wonder. We had discovered an important insight into our daughter: we only needed to take her for a drive in a car when she had colic pain. The only problem was: we didn't have a car.

A few days later, we visited Sheila, an old school friend of Vidya, and her husband Prem. They lived nearby. When we were there Preeti had one of her severe bouts of colic pain. She was still crying when we got up to leave.

'Let me drop you home in my car,' Prem suggested. We thanked him and gladly got into the back seat of his car as his wife joined him in the front.

Preeti stopped crying as soon as the car began to move, but she did not go to sleep. The distance between Prem's house and ours was only a couple of kilometres and he was covering them at a good clip. Preeti was sitting on my lap smiling happily. I rocked her vigorously to induce sleep, but this only seemed to make her giggle more.

'This is your street, right?' asked Prem. Oh no! We had reached home.

'Yes,' I said. 'But don't enter here. There are many potholes on this stretch. Go straight.' I glanced at my daughter. She was wide awake. 'Now that you've taken this road, I want to show you a beautiful temple.'

Vidya jabbed me with her elbow but I ignored her. Preeti needed to be driven a little longer to go to sleep and give us few hours of bliss. But we reached the temple and she was still wide awake. And as Prem brought the car to a halt, she filled up her lungs, ready to let go.

'Don't stop!' I cried. 'The temple is more beautiful if you see it when you drive around it. Ouch!' I added in pain. My wife had just pinched me in my arm.

'What happened?' asked Prem.

'Nothing,' I said, giving Vidya a stern look. She shrugged and, with a smile, turned away.

I was too busy playing tourist guide to wonder what she found amusing. I made Prem go around the temple three times as I pointed out its features. Luckily on the third round, as I described the stones ('brought all the way from Patna,' I wildly made up), Preeti finally dozed off.

'Ok, I think I've shown you enough,' I said. 'You can drop us home now.'

I turned to Vidya after Prem drove off.

'I mesmerised them so well with my description of the temple, they didn't realize I was prolonging the drive. But why did you prod and pinch me?'

'I was trying to tell you that Sheila and Prem visit this temple every Saturday. She told me they've been doing it for the last ten years.'

Getting the full hotel service

Q&P SENT ME TO JAKARTA for meetings with a client. I travelled from Mumbai to Singapore in the morning and waited a few hours there for the short connecting flight; therefore, by the time I arrived at the hotel at 10 pm, I was exhausted and sleepy. My meeting with the client was at 8 am the following morning, for which I would have to leave the hotel at 7 am.

When I entered my sleek, modern-looking room fifteen minutes later, I was afraid of falling asleep if I ate immediately, which would mean either turning up for the client meeting in crumpled clothes or waking up early to iron them. Neither prospect was appealing; so I postponed ordering room service and started looking for the iron in the usual places—wardrobe, desk drawers and bedside table—but couldn't find it. Out of desperation, I even looked in the bathtub, under the bed, and behind the curtains.

At 10.30 pm, I called housekeeping.

'Please face the writing desk and look on the right, sir. You'll see a coin-sized yellow button on the wall. Press it.' I did so and lo! A hidden cupboard, cleverly blended into the wall panel, swung open, revealing an ironing board and iron inside. She continued, with pride in her voice: 'The extra wardrobe space allows you to store eight suits, sir,' and paused expectantly.

'Excellent,' I said. 'This will be very helpful when I buy seven more suits and travel with my full wardrobe.'

By 11 pm, ironing done, I called room service.

'I'd like to order some mushroom soup,' I said, 'if it's vegetarian.'

'Yes, sir! All mushrooms are vegetarian,' the good man assured me. 'They grow on the ground and...'

'I meant the stock,' I cut in.

'Let me check, sir.'

He hung up before I could stop him.

He called again at 11.15 pm. 'We have plenty of mushroom soup in stock; no problem, sir.'

I explained that my question was whether the stock was vegetarian or not. He promised to check again.

'No, take my order!' I screamed. 'If the stock is vegetarian, I'll have mushroom soup. But if it's not vegetarian, get me a garden salad instead. And I'll have the focaccia vegetarian sandwich.'

'Okay, sir. Is that all?'

'Yes. How long will it take?'

'Please allow forty minutes for your freshly prepared, hot meal to reach you, sir.'

My phone rang at 11.30 pm.

'Good news, sir! Not only are the mushrooms vegetarian, the stock is, too. Can I confirm your order: one mushroom soup and one focaccia vegetarian sandwich?'

'Yes.'

'And cancel the garden salad?'

'Yes. How long will it take?'

'Please allow forty minutes for your freshly prepared, hot meal to reach you, sir.'

As I waited, it occurred to me that if I had ordered room service as I entered the room, they could have done the research on the vegetarian nature of the soup while I was ironing my clothes. Forty five minutes later, I rang to enquire about my order. I was put on hold.

'Very sorry, sir,' said the man after I had listened to five minutes of advertising extolling the hotel's services. 'Your order went to room no 1432 instead of 1342!' He paused, perhaps to give me time to roar with laughter; then continued, 'It's coming now.'

The food arrived at 1 am. At 1.10 am, room service called to ask if the food had arrived.

'Yes,' I said. 'I'm eating it now.'

'Wonderful, sir. Perhaps you will fill up the feedback form?' he asked hopefully.

I finished my meal at 1.30 am, requested the operator for a 6 am wake-up call and hit the bed.

I was jerked awake by the ringing phone. I reached for it groggily, noting the time on the bedside clock. It was 1.55 am.

'Room service, sir! Did you enjoy the food?' Taking my silence as affirmation, he continued: 'Can we collect the tray now? And perhaps the feedback form?'

'I placed the tray outside my door, along with the 'Do not disturb' sign, fifteen minutes ago. I was asleep when you called.'

He apologized profusely and promised me I would not be disturbed again.

He was true to his word. I got no more calls after that, including the one to wake me up at 6 am.

'How long will it take to get there?'

TWO DAYS LATER, I WAS keen to be on time for my meeting, having woken up the previous day at 8 am for a meeting that was to start at 8 am. But I was relaxed. Today's meeting was at an offsite venue and scheduled to start only at 10.30 am. But with one thing and another (including a sumptuous buffet breakfast), it was 10 am when I got into the hotel car.

I gave the driver the address and asked him the distance, using the rudimentary Bahasa Indonesia my Indonesia colleagues had taught me the previous day to help me navigate my way by taxi. I had learnt that '*Ja-woo*' meant 'far' but the amount the driver stretched the word, I was told, would give me a better estimate of the distance. For example if he barked out a curt '*Ja-woo*' (like the short '*woof-woof*' of a dog demanding a cookie, they said), it meant my destination was only a few minutes way but if he stretched the second syllable, as in '*Ja-wooooo*' (like the same dog howling at night when it is greeting its mates in the neighbourhood), it meant it was a fair distance.

This time the driver took a deep breath and went '*Ja-woooooooooooooooo*!' for a long time till his lungs were empty.

'Oh no!' I said in dismay. '*Berapa lama* (how long will it take)?'

'*Satu jam* (one hour),' he said.

Not two days in a row, I thought, that too with the same client! I had already been 'caught in a nasty traffic jam' the previous day so I began searching my mind for a different excuse (sudden call from a sick aunt in India?) when the driver brought the car to a halt. We had driven into a compound and he brought the car to a halt at the lobby of an imposing building. We had reached.

I looked at my watch. It was only 10.20 am. I was 10 minutes early!

That day I learnt that Indonesian drivers over-estimate the distance and the time to get there. Their lowest starting bid appeared to be '*satu jam*' (one hour).

The very next week, I learnt that the Indian driver's approach to the same problem is very different. I was in Delhi in a car I had hired for the day. Having finished work at 5.30 pm I got into the car and gave the driver the address of a coffee shop.

'How long will it take?' I asked him. 'I have to meet my friend here at 6 pm.'

'Oh, just five minutes, sir! It's just there.' He pointed vaguely in the north-western direction; then turned to me and gave a broad grin. 'We have plenty of time.'

Five minutes later we had travelled 100 metres and were stuck at a traffic signal.

'Five minutes are over,' I said to the driver. 'And if I turn around, I can see the office building from where we started.'

'This signal is always jammed, sir,' he said. 'But once we clear it, only five minutes.' His voice brimmed with confidence.

'What happened, Suresh?' I asked at 5.45 pm. 'It's fifteen minutes since we started and we're still in Hauz Khas.'

'Very bad traffic today, sir,' he said conspiratorially, as if he were revealing a closely guarded secret. 'Slow traffic till the next signal; after that, just five minutes! The coffee shop is just there.' Again, he pointed jauntily to his front and right.

5.45 pm became 6.00. At 6.10, I called my friend to apologize for my delay but the driver never thought of apologizing for all his glorious 'five minute' estimates.

Finally, he dropped me at the coffee shop at 6.28 pm.

'Here you are, sir. I brought you here in time—' we were thirty minutes late '—but if the traffic had been lighter, I could have done the trip in...'

'In five minutes. Yes, I know,' I said.

An electric guitar for children

I WAS LEARNING THE ROPES OF the advertising business steadily. Today I was with the Q&P team presenting our creative solution to Summer Time, a multinational company specializing in toys for children, for the launch of the company's new electric guitar for children aged 3+. The product was a big hit in the US and the company was gung-ho about its prospects in India, a 'country with a rich history of music,' according to the brief, which also described the guitar as a 'breakthrough product that makes music easy and fun for kids to learn.'

'The child is bored with the toy,' said Faroukh Lokhandwala, the creative lead, pointing to the first scene of his storyboard, 'and throws it away in disgust. He reaches for the new Summer Time electric guitar and…'

'Wait!' said Mahesh Tripathi. 'What toy was the boy playing with?'

Tripathi, the marketing director, was a veteran marketer from the consumer durables industry and had joined Summer Time to lead its marketing charge into India. While he was presumably adept at convincing dealers to order washing machines in bulk, he had not so far demonstrated any panache for advertising.

Well, he is certainly not going to start today, I thought, as I heard his question.

'I don't know,' said Lokhandwala irritably. 'Any toy—say GI Joe.'

'No!' said Tripathi. 'NOT GI Joe! My four-year old boy NEVER gets bored of GI Joe. Come on guys, demonstrate some consumer understanding here.'

'Excellent point, Mahesh,' I said quickly before Lokhandwala said anything foolish. 'We will consult with you separately and feature the right toy that the boy gets bored with.'

'Good, good,' said Tripathi. 'Go on.'

'As he picks up the Summer Time guitar and plucks the strings,' continued Lokhandwala, 'melodious music fills the room. The kid is enchanted. Cut to guitar on the floor and the family dog runs into the room and jumps on the guitar. Immediately…'

'Which breed of dog?' Tripathi wanted to know.

'Which breed do you think is appropriate?' asked Lokhandwala. I beamed at him—the lad was learning fast.

'Labrador,' said Tripathi decisively. 'They always run into the room and jump on stuff.'

'Okay. The Labrador jumps on the guitar and it starts playing beautiful music. The dog gets excited and jumps on it some more: it plays more music. Cut to the boy's dad returning home from work, tired and irritated. When he sees toys all over the living room, he lets out a snarl and kicks them. As he kicks the guitar, it lets out a melodious howl and jumps in the air, lands and rolls, playing beautiful music all the time, enchanting music that changes dad's mood from raspy to mellow. Son walks in, picks up guitar from floor, crawls into dad's lap and continues to play beautiful music. Dog and mom enter room. Everybody is happy. Dissolve to our slogan: 'Music is child's play with Summer Time.' That's it. What do you think?'

We waited. As usual, confronted with approving a piece of advertising, Tripathi looked uncomfortable.

'I don't know,' he said finally. 'It lacks seriousness, you know. Why is the child playing the fool with the guitar in the first place?'

'Children play, Mahesh,' I said. 'And the guitar is meant for the child.'

'Yes but why is he so frivolous? Likewise the dog. In fact, do we need the kid and the dog?'

He began to draw lines through the storyboard.

'How about this?' he said a few minutes later. 'We start with dad entering home, but not kicking the guitar—let's show some respect for the product. He picks it up gently and...'

'But he is in bad mood after a hard day at work,' protested Lokhandwala.

'Or... he is happy after a good day at work,' said Tripathi. 'Let's be positive, people! He plays the guitar, wonderful music happens. Kid comes in; dad teaches kid how to play—now we have some heart-wrenching father-son bonding too—mom enters... everybody's happy. You can have the dog come in too,' he added generously.

'Sorry, I'm five minutes late for my next meeting,' Tripathi continued. 'Why don't you make the changes and come back to present tomorrow—I'll rope in Shyam too.' Shyam Swaroop was his boss and CEO of the Summer Time.

In the taxi back to the office, I soothed Lokhandwala's frayed nerves.

'Rewrite the script as he suggested,' I said. 'But bring the original storyboard along too...'

The next day we presented the revised storyboard to Tripathi and his boss Swaroop.

'...and everyone is happy,' concluded Lokhandwala as he described the delirious last scene with dog, mother, father and child.

'I'm not,' said Swaroop. 'Where's the creative idea, guys? My marketing director could have written the story.'

Before Lokhandwala could say 'He did', I spoke.

'You don't like it?' I said. 'Well, we do have another, slightly different way of doing the story.' I turned to Lokhandwala. 'Did you bring the other storyboard?'

Lokhandwala took out the original storyboard and explained it. Swaroop was pleased with what he saw. And Tripathi was not upset to observe us present the storyboard he had jettisoned. In fact, he too was absorbed in observing Swaroop's reaction.

'Superb!' said Swaroop, when Lokhandwala finished. 'This is great.' He turned to Tripathi. 'Mahesh, you must have seen both storyboards. Why didn't the agency show me the better one first?'

'I'm surprised too,' said Tripathi and fixed me with an unblinking look. 'Tell us why.'

Addressing a change

WHEN I TOOK UP THE offer to move to Q&P Advertising, Vidya was pregnant with our second child. As a direct consequence, I experienced a second change a few months after I started my new job: having our second child, Anand. The lad lived up to his name, maintaining a calm demeanour in the face of adversity. Firstly, he seemed much less troubled by colic pain than his sister had been. (But when I mentioned this to our venerable paediatrician Dr P.M. Samant, he disagreed with me as usual. 'You're just noticing it less,' he said and laughed.) Anand also never complained that we had fewer photograph albums of his—managing to fill only two in the first six months of his life, compared to half a dozen for his sister in half the period—and he even wore Preeti's discarded frocks with alacrity. He was a thorough gentleman, in short.

It was also time for a third change. Vidya and I moved our residence from Juhu to Bandra in Mumbai and I began the painful task of informing various bodies about the change in my address. I expected my private-sector bank to process the change with quick efficiency but that's when I realized that the private sector had inculcated the fine art of bureaucracy from the government.

I set the ball rolling by calling my bank and requesting the woman on the phone to take down my new address, which she did very politely.

'Thank you,' I said, 'Please send all future correspondence to the new address.'

'With pleasure, sir,' she said. 'But you have to write to us giving your old and new address.'

'But you have my old address—you keep sending me mail there. And I just gave you my new address.'

'Yes, sir, we do and you did,' she said. 'But we need it in writing, with your signature.'

I was a little peeved as I had painstakingly spelled out each word of my address ('J as in juxtaposition, U as in unambiguous...' and so on).

'Okay, I'll fax my instructions to you,' I said.

'We cannot accept a fax, sir. Please mail it to this address.' She read it out.

I was tempted to tell her that I needed the bank's address in writing but it would only complicate things because the bank would send its current address to my old address.

'And, sir,' the good woman went on. 'We also need a self-attested bill addressed to you at the new address. It could be a bill for your electricity, or telephone or even gas. We're very flexible.'

'Why?'

'The bank's policy is to be flexible to the customer, sir.'

'I mean, why do you need proof when I'm instructing you in writing?!'

Her training did not include the answer to this question. So I found a phone bill and wrote the bank a letter with my old address, my new address and, to play it safe, the reason for my move.

After ten days I got a standard form reply: my request for a change of address had not been approved. My folly (ticked from a list of misdemeanours): *Failure to provide a self-attested proof of residence.*

I called the friendly woman again but I was not in a friendly mood.

'Surely your bank, while big and powerful, is going beyond its authority in *not approving* my change of address,' I said, 'especially as I'm already staying there?'

'I'm sorry about the wording, sir.' She was as polite as ever. 'But the rules have to be followed.'

'But if my new address is *not approved*,' I said, 'why did you send the letter here? Ha!'

The woman sounded scared as she murmured: 'The letter was sent to your old address, sir, as you'll see in its body. But since I had your new address, I sent a copy there on my own initiative. I don't want to get into trouble, sir.'

'Don't worry—your secret is safe with me. But do you think I'm lying about where I'm staying?'

'No, sir!' she cried, 'You're a good man.'

I was impressed—first she had shown initiative by sending a copy of the letter to my correct address and now she was showing excellent judgement of character. But I still wanted to know why the bank asked that I attest my proof of residence. Surely if I can forge the phone bill, I can easily sign it too?

'I'd still like to speak to someone in charge,' I said.

'Yes, sir!' She sounded relieved, 'You should talk to the Consumer Banking Head.'

'Please connect me to him,' I said.

'Sorry, sir, I can't do that. You need to visit our website, go to Personal Banking, click on the tab My Services and under Downloadable Forms, find the form for Requesting Telephone Appointment, print it, fill it up—in blue or black ink—sign it and send it to… are you ready to take down the address, sir?'

I wasn't. Silently, I hung up.

An ancient civilization in the 21st century

I LANDED EARLY IN THE MORNING at Cairo's international airport. I was there for some advertising conference. I yawned as I got into the hotel limousine: I was groggy after an overnight flight. But in two seconds I was jerked out of languor as the car took off like an unleashed panther, its tires squealing. I tried telling the large Egyptian driver I was in no hurry, but he was busy on his cell phone. Holding it against his ear, he talked loudly, nonchalantly steering with one hand. The speedometer rose to 100 kilometres per hour. Meanwhile he had not buckled up: the vehicle's warning system started going *'ping-ping-ping'* with increasing volume. To compensate, he talked louder.

He disconnected after a few minutes and turned around, grinning broadly.

'Sir, comfortable?' he asked.

'Ping-ping-ping-ping-ping!' went the car.

'Yes, yes,' I said, 'But please look at the road. And wear your seat-belt. And slow down.'

He turned back unhurriedly and clicked his seat-belt (but ignored my third request). I enjoyed tranquillity for about ten seconds before he switched on the radio. A melancholy Arabic dirge filled the car. Starting to protest, I suddenly stopped. I don't know whether her lament was for her lost lover or her stained laundry, but the soulful voice calmed my nerves. I started taking in Cairo in the early morning light.

Dust! I thought. Everything looked dusty. The buildings were worn-out and covered in dust. Speeding cars swept the highway clean but the cars themselves were weather beaten and dusty. The pavement was dusty too. Smiling Egyptians beckoned at me from billboards through a layer of dust. Through the ridges of a dusty bridge, even the graceful Nile seemed covered with dust. A city built on a desert, I thought, never quite rises above its sands.

We screeched to a halt at the Marriott. The driver turned to me hopefully.

'Good driver?'

Since there was no one else nearby, I surmised he was referring to himself. Not having the heart to disagree, I smiled and gave him a few Egyptian Pounds and was rewarded with another huge grin.

Checking in, I nodded in approval at the badge worn by every hotel staff member saying, *YES is the answer. What is the question?* 'Can I have the International Herald Tribune newspaper?' I asked.

'No,' said the receptionist.

I loved Egypt's relaxed custom of starting meetings at 10.30 am (*everything* is laid-back: breakfast starts at 10 and continues till noon, lunch till 5 pm, and dinner till midnight). I was scheduled to speak first. I started my presentation but stopped abruptly—a participant at the front table was lighting a cigarette! Used to people slinking out of buildings and huddling on the pavement to smoke, I waited for someone to rebuke the smoker. Instead *everyone* started lighting up and looking at me with mild curiosity (they don't get agitated in Egypt) as if wondering, 'Granted, he wasn't talking much sense, but why has he stopped?'

I soon learnt that you can smoke everywhere in Egypt: in meeting rooms, corridors, balconies, taxis, bars, restaurants... ashtrays are always at hand. But in scrupulous fairness to non-smokers, you are also allowed to *not smoke* in these places.

That evening we dined in the Marriott's open air lawn—a serene area near the hotel swimming pool, lined with palm trees. The food, served by courteous, smiling waiters, was delicious. It started with spongy Egyptian bread eaten with different condiments. I filled myself with this but, not allowing a full stomach to hinder me, did justice to the rice and vegetables that followed.

On my free day, I visited the Sphinx and the Pyramids at Giza, imposing 5,000-year old structures rising out of the desert. Ancient Egyptian kings, disagreeing that 'you can't take your worldly possessions with you', carried them into their tombs in pyramids whose slopes were believed to facilitate an easy ascent for the erstwhile king to heaven. And at the Egypt Museum, I viewed the treasures from one such tomb, of King Tutankhamun. Four gilded shrines nested one inside the other: the outer three held the pharaoh's stunning jewellery; in the innermost was a stone sarcophagus containing three coffins nested inside each other. The innermost coffin—110 kilograms of solid gold—contained the pharaoh himself (dead, of course).

In the plane flying back home, one question kept nagging me. If they designed the pyramid slopes to provide the king an easy passage to heaven, why did they make it so difficult for the poor fellow to get out of his tomb, having to smash his way out of three coffins and then four gilded shrines?

The professional tennis player

MANAGING AN ACCOUNT IN AN agency, I soon learnt, is about managing and influencing two categories of people, both particularly difficult to influence.

The first category was our clients. The ones I had encountered as a consultant exhibited a more human—or less nasty—side than the ones I met now as an ad agency man. Though in both cases the client pays good money for the services, they feel *privileged* to pay for the consultant but *cheated* to pay for the advertising agency. This is because in their heart, every client believes they are creative and easily capable of writing mind-blowing, heart-wrenching, soul-uplifting advertising for their brand. But because they have hired an ad agency, they are forced to keep their ideas in check and listen to bearded guys in tattered jeans tell them what to do... and pay up for listening.

The second category of people I had to manage as account director was the bearded rascals themselves. They were our creative geniuses who came up with the ideas, wrote the stories, drew the pictures and designed the layouts. When not doing this, they generally lounged around looking dreamy and acting stubborn, especially with anything that the client said. Creative people believe that any idea—or reaction to their idea—from the client is worthless, and they express this belief very clearly... to the account director. They expect the account director to manage the client's stubbornness. In the same way, the client expects the account director to manage the creative people's stubbornness. As an account director I felt like a mild-mannered, gentle slice of tomato placed between two nasty slices of bread that did not get on with each other.

However, I knew one client who was different from his difficult brothers and sisters. Bhaskar Shetty—a marketing manager with Zenith Health, that large multinational company famous for its over-the-counter medicine and baby foods—was soft-spoken and reasonable. He was also a good tennis player (which perhaps explained his kind nature) and I enjoyed interacting with him on the tennis court every Saturday as much as I did interacting with him in the office.

'Would you like to be posted to Singapore?' Prashant Ghosh asked me one day. Apparently there was an account director role in the Q&P's Singapore office and he was offering it to me.

I was excited. 'How come you thought of me for this role?' I asked, wondering which of my leadership traits he would cite. I was open to listening to any of them.

'I didn't,' he said. 'Bhaskar Shetty has been transferred by Zenith to Singapore and he would particularly like you to manage the regional account for their Toddler baby food brand from Q&P's office there. He felt that the continuity would do his brand good.'

'And his tennis game,' I said but only to myself.

That evening I asked Vidya what she thought of the idea of moving to Singapore.

'Why not?' she said. 'Preeti and Anand will love growing up there. Congratulations!'

'Actually it was my tennis prowess that got me this posting,' I said. I gave her the whole story; then I grinned as I thought of something.

'You realize my salary will be higher in Singapore, right?' Vidya nodded. 'And one could say that the reason I'll be getting the extra money is my prowess at tennis, right?'

'Well,' she said, 'in a roundabout sort of way, yes, but if…'

'Enough.' I interrupted her long-winded rambling. '"Yes" was the only answer I wanted to hear. Because that makes me a professional tennis player! I can't wait to tell my dad. He would always point out to me, when he wanted me to study more and play less, that I didn't have what it takes to become a pro.'

A sensible sense of time

VIDYA AND I FOUND IT remarkably easy to settle into Singapore. In the first few days we found that more Tamil is spoken here than in Mumbai; Parle G biscuits and Maggi *masala* flavoured noodles were easily available and Little India definitely lives up to its name. In fact we found everything hunky dory… until we encountered the Singaporean's strange sense of time.

For us in India, time is a loose, arbitrary concept, worn casually like a bathrobe at the poolside on a Sunday. When an Indian says he will do something 'definitely by tomorrow', he means he will get to it in the next few days, God willing. Likewise if he says he observed the full moon 'just yesterday', he means he saw it sometime during the last week (and perhaps it was not really, completely full). And on both occasions, to make matters worse, he will use the same word *kal*, a roomy Hindi term that accommodates both tomorrow *and* yesterday in its meaning.

In India, it is normal to be invited for dinner at 'around 7.30 pm' but actually landing up anywhere close to that time would be considered a severe breach of manners. The hosts would still be cooking dinner or visiting the supermarket for ice or relaxing at the park with the kids. It is customary for the first guest to arrive after 9 pm and the last closer to 11.

Soon after we came here, a Singaporean parent of my son's classmate, who I met at a parent-teacher meeting, invited us home for dinner. 'Come at 7 pm,' he said. 'We've invited two other couples.'

'We should reach his place at about 8.30 pm,' I told my wife on the day of the dinner. 'So we should leave home at 8. That means,' I added, to ensure she understood the gravity of this statement, 'you need to be ready by 7.55.'

'Absolutely,' she said and promptly came out dressed—at 8.45 pm.

It was 9.15 pm when we parked the car at our host's apartment complex. As we reached his door, it opened and we met the other guests. They were leaving after their dinner.

Much embarrassment ensued. I apologized for our tardiness; my wife apologized after me in her inimitable way ('I told Jags we should go earlier but he didn't listen'); our host apologized for not taking my phone number and therefore not calling me (to ask what the devil I was up to); his wife apologized for serving the dinner without us; the four guests individually apologized for eating it and leaving so early. After going around at the rate of one apology per person, an uncomfortable silence descended on the group, and everyone seemed to be looking at me. So I apologized again and we went around one more time.

We might have done it a third time but the host's wife broke the deadlock. 'Why don't you come in and eat? You must be hungry and there's lots of food.'

My wife and I entered their apartment reluctantly, but not as reluctantly as the other guests. Too polite to leave, they sat in the living room looking at us stonily while the good hosts laid the table and took food out of the refrigerator. I could sense their thoughts: *A lovely night ruined, thanks to this idiot*. When the food was ready, we all sat down at the dining table and, under the spotlight glare of six adults, my wife and I ate. I could have entertained everyone with a couple of funny anecdotes about life in India that I had in my repertoire but I felt the mood was not right. One of the guests was constantly drumming the table—'eat fast, eat fast, eat fast', her fingers seemed to say—and another kept looking at his watch. So my wife and I ate silently... and at a frantic clip.

Soon we were ready to leave, as were the other table-drumming, watch-watching guests. After we had said our goodbyes and thrown a few more apologies at everyone, I turned to my wife.

'Phew!' I said, 'Next time, we go ten minutes earlier than the time he calls us.'

But for some odd reason, the gentleman didn't call us again. The only explanation I can think of is that he must have lost his cell phone and with it, my phone number, which I had taken care to give him that day.

The dual-country driver

'IF YOU CAN DRIVE IN India, you can drive anywhere in the world,' my father would say with remarkable authority for a man who had never set foot outside India's shores.

When I moved to Singapore, I thought the broad, smooth roads looked easy enough to navigate. Then I noticed something peculiar: they were painted with colourful lines. The white ones were dashed or continuous and the yellow ones were single or double but some of them, instead of following the straight and narrow path, went zigzag down the road, like my college friend Balasubramanium after a few drinks.

Disconcerted by this display of geometry, I cornered a Singaporean colleague.

'What are these lines?' I asked, pointing to the road.

'Lanes?' he said.

Feeling bad for the poor fellow's hearing, I raised my voice.

'NOT LANES. LINES!'

'Don't shout,' he said, rubbing his ears. 'Those *lines* demarcate *lanes*. You have to drive within your lane.'

'I get my own lane?' I was impressed.

Shaking his head, he took me for a drive in his car to educate me. Apparently I had to stay in the leftmost lane and use the indicator to switch lanes to overtake. So restrictive! In India, we drive on whichever part of the road we like and, if an opportunity for overtaking presents itself (as sometimes happens between 1 and 5 am), we do it in any direction—right, left, up or down.

My colleague continued: 'On a lane bordered by a *continuous* white line, you may not change lanes under any circumstances.'

With my trademark cunning, I thought of a loophole: 'What if I suddenly see a pothole in front?'

'What's a pothole?'

'I'll show you,' I said, pained by his ignorance, 'Keep driving.'

He did but, though I made him change lanes several times, I couldn't show him a pothole. Finally I had to acknowledge his ignorance was based on bliss: there are no potholes on Singapore roads.

He continued: 'A single yellow line signals it's the edge of the road; a double yellow line means you can drop someone off but cannot park; a zigzag line means you cannot even drop someone and a double zigzag...'

'Let me guess,' I said, 'You cannot even dream about thinking of contemplating the idea of perhaps stopping.'

'Don't you have lanes in India?'

'While driving late at night, I have noticed a few lines on some Mumbai roads.'

Now he looked perplexed. 'They draw the lines at night and wipe them off in the morning?'

'No, but they're invisible during day because we drive all over them. The lines are only for fun.'

He graciously invited me to practise on his car, so I got behind the wheel. I found it easy enough to stay in my lane but soon came behind a car. I pressed the horn a few times.

'What are you *doing*?' my friend screamed.

'Sounding the horn,' I explained, honking a few more times.

He caught my hand. 'Stop, *please*!'

I learnt that you don't honk to tell the fellow that you're behind him: he already knows it, having seen you in one of his side mirrors (the ones we tuck in carefully in India to prevent passing motorists from clipping them off).

Soon I learnt to drive in my lane... on smooth roads that did not have potholes. I learnt to use the rear-view mirrors and not to use the horn. But in many ways I missed driving in India's madly busy roads, where pedestrians, cycles, scooters, cars and buses jostle companionably for space. I remember that when traffic came to a standstill, I could pass time by buying a vada pao to eat or a book to read from mobile merchants always nearby. And the road gave me moments of ecstasy that lasted. After a lousy day at the office I would retire for the night not thinking dark thoughts about my frustrating meeting, but reminiscing happily about my neat manoeuvre that morning when, in the split second before the signal turned green, I squeezed into the narrow space ahead of the Mercedes Benz on my right and, horn blazing, raced ahead in triumph and glory.

A king-sized city

I WAS VISITING Q&P'S HEADQUARTERS FOR a series of meetings and the long flight from Singapore to Chicago (via San Francisco) was coming to an end.

'We're approaching Chicago, folks,' the captain cheerfully announced. I perked up immediately and paid attention.

The captain continued his happy announcement. 'Folks, you have a few minutes to visit the toilet, but don't worry if you can't: O'Hare is a modern airport, equipped with toilets!'

We laughed politely.

'It's a bright day,' he continued. 'Clear skies and a ground temperature of -18^0 Celsius.'

I laughed politely again. But my thin American neighbour did not join me.

'You missed the joke,' I said, 'He said *minus* 18^0.'

'Chicago does get cold in winter,' he said, looking puzzled.

'You mean it? It is *actually* -18^0 outside?' He nodded.

I stopped laughing. In fact, I think I stopped breathing. The only warm clothing I had brought in my efficient hand-carry suitcase was a tracksuit bottom and a light sweater. I was already wearing both items because I find aircraft interiors cold. And I was about to step out into weather 40 degrees colder! I took my jeans out of my suitcase.

'To help me tackle the cold outside,' I explained to my neighbour as I pulled the jeans up over my tracksuit bottom.

'Ha, ha, ha!' he roared, displaying more enthusiasm than the situation demanded. 'That's like lighting a candle in a hurricane. It's like drilling for oil with a toothpick. It's like building a house…'

'I got it,' I said coldly, 'But I forgot it's winter here and didn't bring anything warmer.'

'You forgot it's winter in Chicago?!' He laughed some more. 'Oh man! That's like forgetting there's sand in the Sahara, or water in the Pacific Ocean, or grass in…'

'Yes.' I interrupted this Emperor of Analogies, 'I'll buy myself something in Chicago.'

Four seconds after exiting the airport, my ears were numb, my nose and eyes were watering and my fingers felt like icicles. Luckily the Hertz bus arrived a few seconds later and it was comfortably heated. Observing fellow travellers shed four layers of clothing, I tried to smirk, but my face was still frozen. I felt I had thawed by the time I left the bus and entered my rental car, which had been thoughtfully warmed beforehand. By the time I drove to my hotel in downtown Chicago, I felt like freshly ejected toast. But when the doorman calmly told me the hotel charged $40 a day for parking, I felt chilly again.

'$40?' I said, 'Will the car get a room with an attached bath for that?'

'No, sir,' he replied seriously, 'But you can take the car out as many times a day as you like, at NO ADDITIONAL CHARGE.'

Though he made it sound like a deal unrivalled in the history of retailing, I wasn't impressed.

After my meeting the first day, I paid handsome prices for gloves, a scarf and a winter coat at the mall, with glorious '70% off on our summer collection' banners mocking me from the neighbouring aisles. Wearing them I exited the mall and stepped into Michigan Avenue, Chicago's commercial hub, where past and present merge with harmony. Grand granite structures a century old stand next to today's sleek glass and steel buildings. Except for the cars driving on the wrong side of the road, I could have been in London.

I saw a building bearing the name American Girl and walked in out of curiosity. My mind boggled: it was a doll shop on three storeys! Around me were pretty dolls, tall dolls, blonde dolls and musical dolls; hard dolls, soft dolls and dolls made of special fabric; branded Barbie dolls, historical dolls, dolls from literature and dolls from around the world. Then there were accessories for dolls: clothes, hats, make-up kits, school bags, and bedrooms. There were books about the dolls; a theatre showing movies about the dolls and a café... wait a minute, was this to *feed* the dolls?! Thankfully, no. At the café tables, small girls sat with their mothers. I then realized I was surrounded by mothers and daughters; the occasional father tagging along looked out of place but not as much as I did, a lone middle-aged man gazing open-mouthed at the dolls.

The next day, a Q&P colleague invited me to play tennis. I gazed at him in admiration.

'No way, Bill,' I said, 'I can barely walk outdoors in this cold. No question of playing tennis.'

He explained that it was an indoor court, so of course I agreed and met him at the East Bank Club, a deceptively modest building resembling a warehouse but housing 14 indoor tennis courts, a swimming pool, a gymnasium the size of a hockey field, several squash and racquetball courts, and—for the armchair-inclined—lounges, bars, and restaurants. The tennis courts, being protected from weather year-long, were perfectly smooth. Therefore the ball bounce is as true as winter's first snowflake. Playing was a pleasure, but I missed not being able to use my standard excuses for a desultory performance—wind, bad bounce, sun in the eyes or sudden car honking.

After the tennis game, I walked into a Starbucks near my hotel, reflecting on the large sizes of everything in USA: a doll shop as big as a mall; a lake that resembles the ocean and an indoor club the size of modest agricultural farm.

'What size, sir?'

I stared uncomprehendingly at the Starbucks options and ventured, 'Venti?'

Seeing her reach for a bucket-like cup, I quickly corrected myself. 'No, smaller… much smaller.'

'Ok, 'Tall' then.' She took out another cup.

'No, that's still too big,' I said.

'Sorry, sir,' she said. 'This is the smallest size we have.'

A 'small' drink of 350 ml fits well with everything else in this king-sized city, I thought, as I walked into the hotel.

The traits of a successful copy writer

As an executive in the advertising agency, I often got quizzed about my job. The questions usually displayed a thoroughly misguided idea that the ad agency business was all fun and games. For example: Was it true that all advertising executives start drinking at 11 am every day? How often do you dine with leading film stars? What's your golf handicap?

But during my trip to America, I got a different type of question from my nephew, who was doing his undergraduate programme in creative design in the University of Chicago. He visited me at my hotel and in a very earnest voice, asked: 'How can I become a good copy writer?'

I looked at him in surprise. I had last seen him when he was boy of ten. To make a good impression on his uncle, he had come to meet me in an immaculate suit, his face freshly shaven and his hair combed neatly. The scent from his cologne wafted through my hotel room.

'You see,' he continued. 'I've always been meaning to put this question to a solid marketer with a sound knowledge of the ad industry.'

I smiled modestly.

'But I couldn't find anyone,' he continued. 'So I'm asking you. How can I be a successful copy writer?'

'First,' I said, 'You need to dress properly. Your sophisticated suit makes you look very dapper... for a banker. But it strikes the wrong note for an agency creative. You need to look scruffy and unkempt always and, from time to time, wild and desperate. Do you have an old pair of jeans?'

He nodded.

'That's a great starting point. Tear it in a few places and roll it in mud. Find a T-shirt that matches; on second thoughts, make it one that does not. Bundle them up and stuff them into a drawer overnight so they're suitably crumpled by morning. And I can see you own a very good razor: throw it away—you won't need it again.'

He took out an elegant diary and pen and began to write down what I'd told him.

'Write your notes now,' I continued, 'but after today get yourself a well-worn sketch pad—put it in the washing machine with your clothes once—and a half-chewed pencil stub.'

He wrote furiously.

'Once you turn up in your office like this,' I said, 'everyone will know you're serious. And at the client's, when you show up ten minutes late (as you always should), your account executive will show you off like a prized office possession. The client will be blindingly bowled over. With your appearance sorted out, you're 85 percent of your way to being a successful copy writer.'

I saw him writing '85% - Appearance'. It was a pleasure instructing such an attentive student.

'The next 10 percent depends on your behaviour. Follow two simple rules, worth 5 percent each. Rule Number 1: No one other than a copy writer officially working in the creative department can ever have a creative idea. It just

'With your appearance sorted out, you're 85% of your way to being a successful copy writer.'

cannot happen. If a suit—the friendly term for account people like me—suggests a creative approach, look at her coldly and say, "Do I try to help you get the client estimate approved on time?" If the idea comes from the planner, simply snort.'

'What if it comes from the client?'

'It often will. The client thinks he understands his brand and its consumer and will therefore leap enthusiastically into creative waters, splashing everyone and making a mess. But he is also touchy by nature and disinclined to react favourably to any of the above responses. Simply say, 'Interesting idea' in a bland tone and nod briefly. Don't use any other adjective—"good" will give him unneeded encouragement. "Interesting" is a diplomatic way of saying "stupid".'

He wrote. I continued:

'And at the next meeting, be prepared with a reason why his idea, though interesting, won't work. The best method is to find that it has been used before. This can always be done if you stretch your search wide enough and, once you've found something vaguely similar, stretch your imagination hard enough to interpret them as "one and the same". Do this a few times and the client will gradually reduce his creative contributions to a manageable trickle.'

'Now,' I said, 'Rule Number 2: Always defend your idea to death even if it's dumb. If the client says it feels wrong, tell him the hallmark of a brilliant idea is that it feels wrong initially. (Don't tell him this is also the hallmark of a disastrous idea.) If he gives you an objective reason for his opinion and backs it with data, tell him that creativity is a nebulous, lofty concept that should not be subject to the same statistical rigour as, say, his brand's trailing 12-month sales trend, and that he should react with his gut. Referring to his gut, he can either say it feels right, which is great, or it feels wrong, in which case you know what to say. And if he garnishes your idea with a sprinkle of his own creativity, refer to Rule Number 1.'

'And that's it, my friend,' I said when he finished writing, 'Off you go into the land of creativity!'

'But what about the final 5 percent?' he asked.

'Oh, that? Some people feel a good creative person should develop stimulating new ideas that bring freshness to the brand. I don't think it's important but, just as a cushion, I've left 5 percent... if you have the time and inclination, go for it.'

Talk in America as Americans do

I ALWAYS KNEW THAT IT IS very painful trying to communicate in English to a native of China who speaks Mandarin. But on my trip to the USA, I discovered that it is equally difficult communicating in English to a native of America who speaks American.

I was on a domestic flight from Chicago to Madison to spend two days with an old school friend before heading home via San Francisco. I was seated next to a large American with a large voice and, I soon discovered, an even larger laugh.

'Drink, sir?' The flight attendant was on the aisle beside us with the trolley.

'Whisky and soda,' I said. She nodded and looked enquiringly at my neighbour.

'Copy that!' he said. I was baffled. Surely she would point out to him that she was in no position to copy anything as she was in the middle of dishing out drinks and therefore not carrying a notebook and pencil.

But she said, 'Sure!' and poured him a whisky and soda.

He took a huge sip, grinned and asked me where I was from.

'Singapore,' I said.

'What a ridiculous place!' He let out a guffaw so loud, his tray table trembled.

'Singapore,' I said coldly, 'is a very nice country.'

'Yes, I've been there.' he said. 'It's awesome! It's beautiful! It's ridiculous!'

Oh! It was a compliment. Feeling less miffed, I continued, 'Yes, I've lived there for eleven years and love it. It's modern, clean and safe.'

'You can say that again,' he said.

'I'VE... LIVED... THERE... FOR... 11... YEARS... AND... LOVE... IT,' I repeated, speaking loudly and slowly, 'IT'S... MODERN... CLEAN... AND... SAFE.' He nodded encouragingly, so I went on: 'Everything works. Even when traffic is slow, it moves at a fast clip compared to Los Angeles, for example.'

'You can say that again,' he said; then, seeing me fill my lungs, hastily added: 'No, I don't mean repeat it. We're on the same page.'

This was impossible because neither of us had a book open, but before I could pursue the point, the attendant was back and he was ready. She refilled his glass and turned to me.

'What about you, sir? Are you good?'

I was a little embarrassed by the sudden personal question.

'Well, I think I am, most of the time. But not always... the other day, for example, I downloaded a pirated video.'

'Very interesting, sir,' she said, looking bewildered, 'But would you like another drink or are you good?'

When she had gone, my neighbour said, 'You're not understanding us. Let me learn you some American phrases.'

'Let me *teach* you some American phrases,' I said before I could stop myself, years of correcting my children's grammar automatically kicking in.

'But you hardly know any!'

'Sorry, I meant you should say, "Let me *teach* you, not *learn* you."'

'Oh, my bad,' he said.

I waited but he didn't finish the sentence. While I was wondering whether he meant his bad *comprehension* of English or his bad *back* or the bad *plumbing* in his house, he spoke again.

'If you travel to America often, you need to jump on the bandwagon of Americanisms.'

He explained that this was yet another Americanism meaning to join the movement.

I liked the phrase and decided to employ it at the first opportunity, which came the very next day. I had spent the morning with my friend NLM Krishna. After lunch he had dropped me at the mall and arranged to meet me at a pub after attending a meeting. I was already seated at the pub when he joined me at 6 pm. I waved him over.

'Hi Krishna,' I said, 'I'm having a drink. Why don't you jump on the bandwagon?'

'What?' he said.

'Join me for a drink.'

'I'm on the wagon.'

'No, you're getting this all wrong,' I said. 'You're supposed to jump on the bandwagon and join me.'

'But I'm already on the wagon,' he said, 'because I'm off alcohol. But wait... shouldn't I then be *off* the wagon?'

'I don't have a clue what you're talking about,' I said.

'Okay, let me use a non-American phrase: I'm totally into tea nowadays.'

'What!?'

'Sorry, I meant I'm totalling the tea.'

'I'm still clueless.'

'Sorry again,' he said. 'I've got it now! I'm a teetotaller nowadays.'

'Oh, are you?' I said. 'Well, I need a drink. My mind is reeling.'

'So is mine. You know what? I'm going to get off my wagon and jump on your bandwagon. Get me that drink. And for God's sake, let's switch to speaking in Tamil.'

Flying travails

DOMESTIC FLIGHTS WITHIN THE UNITED States are seldom exhilarating… or even comfortable. But this particular domestic flight from Madison to San Francisco (from where I had to get a connection back to Singapore) was psychologically painful.

The last time I had travelled on this airline, I had been served nothing to eat for the entire five hours—it was bad. However, on the occasion before that, I had been served a meal, which was worse. So this time, with cunning foresight, I bought a pizza to take along. During check-in, my request for a seat in the emergency exit row, which I routinely make without much hope, was surprisingly granted.

When we boarded the plane, two flight attendants stood in the gangway to welcome us. The leader was a six-foot brunette. Her uniform, probably tailored before she took up body-building, accentuated her rippling muscles. With hands on hips and eyebrows puckered in a frown, she watched us board. We slunk past, avoiding eye contact. As we reached our seats, she helped us store our luggage by barking instructions from where she stood: 'sir! You in the blue shirt! Put your suitcase lengthwise. Now keep moving! And you in the black shirt! Move your bag to the left…'

The other flight attendant was much younger, a mere girl of about fifty, less muscular but markedly grumpier.

As I stowed my bags ('Put it deeper... push!') and clambered over the legs of a thickset man at the aisle, my joy of getting the emergency exit row evaporated: in this aircraft, the row had no extra leg room. Instead it had no window seat, affording extra leg room to the person in the *next* row, who had already stretched his legs out luxuriously.

Soon the aircraft was moving. The captain's cheery welcome boomed through the speakers. He thanked us for choosing his airline, apologized for the long taxiing ('Don't worry, folks, we will fly you to San Francisco—we're not driving the whole way') and made droll remarks about the weather. Having heard his colleagues on previous occasions, I'm convinced this airline's pilots' course includes a full section on Humorous Public Speaking.

Meanwhile our flight attendants, Commander and Grumps, began the demonstration of the use of oxygen mask and other paraphernalia with bored, mechanical movements accompanying the bored, mechanical voice on the intercom. As the voice droned on about air bags and water landings, I was overcome with lassitude and my eyelids grew heavy.

The next thing I remember is a heavy hand shaking my shoulder violently.

'Yes, yes... what?' I spluttered, jerking awake.

'Did you hear the safety announcement, sir?' Commander's face was four inches from mine.

'Eh? Yes, of course.'

'And, as you're seated at the exit row, are you prepared to perform the functions if required?'

I nodded.

'What are they?'

'Pardon?'

'What are the functions you may be required to perform?'

'Oh, the usual ones, you know…' I said.

'Yes, sir, *I* know. But do *you* know? Can you tell me what they are?'

Commander's strong voice carried across the aircraft. Conversations ceased as everyone listened to us.

I muttered something in nervous embarrassment.

'Speak up, sir! None of us can hear you. Can we?' She looked around in challenge, then turned back to me. 'You didn't hear a word… you were fast asleep, weren't you?'

I nodded. Magnanimously, Commander did not pinch my ears; with a terse admonishment never to do it again, she turned away. Relief swept over me and my fellow passengers. Someone seated behind me thumped my back and a group of schoolgirls nearby clapped.

Once we were airborne, the attendants brought out the drinks trolley. The portly gentleman beside me asked for cranberry juice.

'I don't have any cranberry juice left on the trolley… sir,' said Grumps.

I expected him to change his request, apologizing for his effrontery, but the man was bold.

'Please get it from the galley.'

'I'll get back to you,' said Grumps.

She never did. As I sipped my Coca Cola, I could feel my neighbour's baleful glare on my neck. I badly wanted my pizza with my drink but it was in the overhead bin. The thought of making my disgruntled neighbour get up and stand in the aisle while I retrieved it was too daunting. And the thought of pressing the call button to summon Commander or Grumps to pass me the pizza was bloodcurdling.

I looked up at the television screen. I think they were showing a western film. Or it could have been a documentary about horses. Or crocodiles. Sitting ten feet behind the ten inch screen, I couldn't be sure.

For the next three hours, I sat bolt upright (my chair's recline function was not working) thinking alternatively about my confrontation with Commander and the pizza sitting tantalizingly close above me. As we landed in San Francisco, I trotted out of the aircraft thinking that the only way I could enjoy flying within the US would be if I could do it without using a plane.

The disease that is mobile

On the way back to Singapore from San Francisco, we encountered a thunderstorm that treated our aircraft the way a chef treats a salad. As we were tossed up, down and sideways, lightning flashed outside the windows. But despite the turbulence outside, I felt inner peace because no one around me was using their mobile phones. The sight of people separated from their technological avatars, simply sitting, talking to their neighbour or reading took me back to the halcyon days of my youth.

Unfortunately even long flights across continents have to come to an end. The moment we landed in Singapore, mobile mania was in full swing. Everyone pulled their phones out of bags and pockets, switched them on hurriedly, and—like addicts finding the drug they had been denied for two days. People used their phones while walking, waiting at immigration and collecting luggage. At the exit they joined people waiting for them, using *their* mobile phones.

In the taxi drive home, I saw a woman, apparently sane, boldly crossing the road while talking on her phone, oblivious to the cars on the road, cars filled with people talking on *their* mobile phones. I smiled at the sight of a man driving alone in the car beside my taxi, talking animatedly, making faces and gesticulating with his hands: twenty years ago, I might have reported him.

The next morning I was enjoying a game of tennis with my client and tennis buddy Bhaskar Shetty. In the crucial seventh game of the set, I was serving at 40-15. As I tossed the ball up, Shetty said, 'Hang on, Jags. Got to take this.' I had heard nothing, but his ears, tuned to his beloved instrument, had picked up its feeble ring tone coming from the bottom of his tennis bag lying on the court-side.

When he returned, I double-faulted, lost the game, and then the set.

'Who called you during the game?' I asked him as we sat at the court-side, sipping water.

'My son.' he said. 'He wanted to know if I had his football.'

Later that day, over lunch with my colleague Suraj Varma I described the villainy of Shetty.

'So the ball is in air—here,' I said, stretching out my hand with a fork in it, 'and I'm bending my body to serve at 40-15, when Shetty stops me from the other side of the net. You know what he says?'

'Hang on, I've got to take this,' said Varma.

'Exactly!' I was thrilled at his perspicacity. 'How did you guess?'

He brought his open palm four inches in front of my face. 'Hang on, Jags!' he said more sharply. 'Hello darling,' he continued, but not to me. He was cooing into the phone.

It was his wife. They talked for five minutes in a leisurely fashion, starting with endearments like 'I love you' and 'I love you too' (his wife had one of those voices that did not require a speaker phone at the other end to be heard by people in the vicinity). He then asked about her programme for the rest of the day ('A visit to the spa before picking up our daughter at school.') and promised to be home for dinner. They discussed the menu (She: 'Eggplant bharta, dal, and roti'. He: 'Excellent, I love your simple but tasty cooking.' She: 'I know, that's why I made it.' He: 'I love you.' She: 'I love you too').

Finally he hung up and, without a trace of apology said: 'Haan, you were saying?'

'Nothing,' I said.

'That was my wife,' he said, unnecessarily. 'What would life be like without the mobile phone?'

I wanted to tell him that, without the mobile phone, I would have won the set this morning and talked about it over lunch instead of failing to do both, but he was still speaking.

'The phone helps me keep track of my children, receive people at the airport and call my wife while driving. I can make calls anytime to anyone from anywhere. How did we ever live our lives without the mobile phone?'

'Quite well,' I said. 'We kept track of our children by looking out of the window because children used to play outdoors in those days. We pre-arranged meeting points at the airport. We drove without talking. Yes, we could *not* make calls anytime to anyone from anywhere. But equally...'

'Hang on, I've got to take this,' said Varma, pulling his phone out of his pocket again.

'... we could not get calls anytime, anywhere and from anyone,' I finished to myself.

I was reminded of my own eloquent speech two days later. My wife answered my mobile phone and told my friend I was in the bathroom.

'Is he bathing?' he wanted to know.

'No,' said Vidya.

'Then?'

'He is...er... otherwise engaged,' she said.

'Then please quickly ask him if the store he recommended is in Sim Lin Tower or Sim Lin Square. I'm approaching both buildings now and need to park at the right one.'

Reunion with Q&P Mumbai

I COULD SEE THAT MY AMERICAN colleague and managing director of Q&P Asia Chris Skinner was excited to be visiting India for the first time. We were travelling to Mumbai to meet our colleagues in Q&P Mumbai to discuss an exciting opportunity—pitching for Gronollers' ready-to-drink (RTD if you want to sound like a marketing man) juice business in Asia. Q&P handled many Gronollers' brands in India but not in any other part of the world. Since Gronollers was happy with the work Q&P did for them in India, they had invited the agency to pitch for their Jolly Juice range of RTD drinks in Asia. Jolly Juice could pave the way for more Gronollers brands coming to the agency so Skinner wanted to leave no stone unturned in this pitch. Therefore he consulted with Prashant Ghosh, CEO of Q&P India, and they agreed that a face-to-face meeting in Mumbai was the best way to pass on India's years of experience in dealing with Gronollers.

'Wow! Is the city crowded or what?!' said Skinner as we exited the bustling Mumbai airport and got into the car arranged by Q&P Mumbai. 'Watch out!' he yelled to the driver a few seconds later.

Without slowing down, the driver had entered a stream of traffic on the main road. Skinner braced himself for a crash but of course there was none. Instead the traffic miraculously parted to accommodate our car. The driver, taking Skinner's cry as an invitation to talk, began to describe Mumbai in halting English.

'Sahar airport very near Hotel Leela,' he said. As he talked, he calmly squeezed the vehicle into any gap (real or imaginary) in the traffic, interrupting himself to curse when someone squeezed ahead of him. Both happened regularly. It was less a drive than a battle to squeeze-in more often than be-squeezed-out; a battle involving cars, taxis, buses, trucks, auto-rickshaws, motorcycles, bicycles and even pedestrians; a battle where everyone was taking what they could without giving an inch.

'Is it always like this?' asked Skinner. He was leaning forward, clutching the top of the seat in front of him with both hands. I could see a bead of nervous perspiration on his brow. 'Or is everyone in a particular hurry today?'

'No one is ever in a hurry in India,' I explained.

'Then why the jostling? And why the incessant honking?'

I had so naturally acclimatized myself to Indian driving conditions that I had not noticed the honking.

'Oh, that's just for fun,' I said. 'When we are taught driving in India, we're told to press the horn as often as the clutch. As for the jostling, it's a game, with a simple rule: if you manage to squeeze your nose into a space, you're allowed to follow with the rest of your vehicle. Relax!' I said as he grimaced when the scooter next to his window suddenly accelerated and squeezed into a one-foot space that had momentarily appeared in front of our car. 'Turn towards me. Don't look at the road.'

Skinner followed my advice and, though he did not completely relax, at least he stopped shuddering every few minutes.

We met our Q&P Mumbai colleagues for dinner at 9 pm at the hotel's restaurant ('Isn't that late?' asked Skinner. 'Not at all,' I assured him.).

'Good to see you again, Jags,' said Prashant Ghosh.

'Likewise,' I said, shaking his soft pudgy hand. I remembered Ghosh fondly, having enjoyed bananas with him on several occasions after that first day of joining Q&P and learning about his policy of 'bananas in every office' (thank God, that madness had not caught on in Q&P outside India).

'I asked Skinner to bring you for this meeting because you've worked at Gronollers, right?'

'Well, when I was at IIMA, I did my summer internship there.'

'That's more than enough,' said Ghosh. 'Two months in the client's shoes—your insights will be invaluable.'

'Let's meet early in the morning, gentlemen,' said Ghosh at 1 am, after many drinks and a heavy dinner.

Skinner was seated next to me. 'I guess I can do an 8 am start,' he murmured to me in a low voice.

'Yes!' continued Ghosh, 'Definitely an early morning start is called for. So—' he flamboyantly turned his wrist and flicked his sleeve up to uncover his watch '—how about meeting at the office around 11 am?'

As we walked to the elevators to take us to our rooms, Skinner said to me, 'I didn't realize he meant early afternoon.'

'He didn't,' I said and explained that 11 am was early morning for the advertising industry in India.

Preparing for a pitch

THE NEXT DAY, ON SKINNER'S insistence we met at the lobby at 10.30 am and were in a taxi a few minutes later. We reached the Q&P office by 10.50 am and were greeted by a bunch of bananas hanging from the wall. Behind it, the friendly receptionist seemed surprised to see us.

But Skinner seemed more surprised to see the bananas. He touched one gingerly.

'Go ahead—take one,' the receptionist said encouragingly. She then gave him the Leo Burnett-apple-versus-Q&P-banana story. Then she said: 'Mr Ghosh isn't here yet. But let me show you to the conference room.'

She led us through the office—very few desks were occupied ('It's still early,' I explained to Skinner)—and into a large conference room and brought us coffee.

By 11.20, we had finished our coffee and I had visited the toilet.

Ghosh walked into the conference room at 11.25 and shook hands with us. 'Make yourselves comfortable,' he added unnecessarily considering we had been sitting comfortably in our chairs for the last half hour, 'I'll be with you in a few minutes—let me also round up the others.'

After he left, people began trickling in at a desultory pace. At 11.40, Ghosh entered the room again.

'Okay, is everyone here?' he said.

'Abhinav Roy just called,' said someone (Roy was the creative director on the Gronollers account), 'to say he's caught in traffic.'

'That means he has just woken up,' said Ghosh. 'Let's begin without him. Shall we start by reviewing the pitch put together by the planners?'

'Before that,' I said, turning to Skinner. 'Is the pitch in our office or Gronollers'?'

'Funny you should ask,' he said. 'They specifically asked if we would host the pitch in our office. I wondered why.'

'I'll tell you why,' I said. 'They want to see if we're using their brands in our premises. So the first thing to do is to ensure the soap in the toilet is a Gronollers brand—I suggest you get Cuddles, the soft-on-hands-hard-on-germs hand wash product.'

'But we're pitching for their RTD business,' said Skinner. 'Not soaps.'

'Your point being?'

'Okay, I'll ask Angelina to get Cuddles soap for the men's room.' He made a note in his pad.

'And the ladies' room,' I said.

'But the three people coming—the managing director, marketing manager and consumer research person—are all male,' said Skinner.

'Gronollers executives check toilets automatically wherever they go. And it is as common for Gronollers' men to step into a ladies' toilet for a quick check as it is for a Gronollers woman to check the men's toilet if they know it's unoccupied.'

'Got it,' said Skinner, scribbling some more.

'Also tell Angelina to ensure the toilet paper—in both toilets—is Flamingo, Gronollers' brand.'

'Why?' said Skinner. 'Once the toilet paper is in the roll, there's no branding on it!'

I looked at him with pity. The man had a lot to learn about the Gronollers culture. 'Any Gronollers executive can recognize all the major toilet paper brands by feeling it with their fingers. And those who have worked on Flamingo don't even need to touch the paper—they can recognize the brand by looking it from a distance of eight feet. The training programme called P-VIS (paper visual identity system) includes a standard eight-feet brand-recognition test.'

I continued: 'Obviously you will serve Jolly Juice during refreshments, along with Wisp crisps?'

Skinner's look suggested that this thought had not occurred to him.

'Gronollers hasn't launched Wisp crisps in Singapore,' he said.

'Then import a few packs,' I said. 'We can carry some of their Indian products back with us.'

'But aren't we overdoing it?'

I explained that it was impossible to overdo the usage of Gronollers brands in the presence of a Gronollers' executive.

'In fact, when we get into the pitch,' I said, 'we should casually mention these brands. For example, if we're talking about home consumption of RTC, we can say: "The trend is for families to stock juice in their refrigerators, just as they stock Gung-ho peanut butter and Shakespeare margarine."'

'On that note,' said Skinner. 'Can we now get to the pitch presentation now?'

I agreed and turned to Ghosh.

'Of course,' he said. 'But it's almost 1 pm. Let's break for lunch.'

A fraternity of fatness

VIDYA BEGAN HER CRUSADE OF getting me to control my weight early in our marriage, leading me to believe that my weight problem has something to do with my eating (in excess) and exercising (in moderation). After moving to Singapore, she became even more vigilant. For example, when I particularly enjoyed something to eat, she would ask me to desist having a third helping. And when I put up my feet to watch an enthralling television programme, she would suggest I visit the gym.

Then one day I read an article that clearly stated that my weight problem had nothing to do with me. The fault lay with my friends. Apparently fatness breeds fatness in the fraternity. Obesity spreads like conjunctivitis from friend to mate to chum. I realized that if I was not lithe and lissom like a fishing rod (which I was not), the fault was with my not-so-slim pals.

I read the article on my computer with rising excitement and carefully printed out the relevant portion. That evening I approached my wife with the paper in my hand and a smug grin on my face.

'Now I know why I'm not able to lose weight,' I said, 'You keep insisting it's because I don't exercise enough.'

'And eat too much,' she said.

'Exactly. That's what *you* say. But today I discovered that my weight has nothing to do with anything I do. It's because my friends are obese. Read what Gina Kolata wrote in the New York Times.'

I quietly handed her the paper and watched with satisfaction as she read the section I had selected:

'In analyzing the Framingham data, Dr Christakis and Dr Fowler found that friends, and friends of friends, had similar levels of obesity, but neighbours did not. Dr Christakis and Dr Fowler proposed a few possible explanations... The third explanation, and the one that garnered so much attention, was contagion. Dr Christakis and Dr Fowler focussed on this as a cause of obesity, saying that they could estimate its effect and that it was large. They theorized that a person's idea of an acceptable weight, or an acceptable portion size, changes when he sees how big his friends are or how much they eat.'

'So,' I said when she finished, 'the problem is not me. It's the stout company surrounding me. For example...'

I began to name friends who carry a lot of weight, literally. But she interrupted me, her eyes back on the paper.

'Hang on,' she said. 'It says they proposed "a few possible explanations". You seem to have cut out the first two. Why didn't you give me the full article to read?'

'Oh, the rest was just technical stuff that would've bored you,' I said airily. 'The point is these two renowned doctors are very gung-ho about the third explanation.'

She insisted on going online to access the full article. When she came back a few minutes later, she was smiling.

'You didn't tell me that many scientists are sceptical about the findings of Christakis and Fowler,' she said. 'Let me read out something from the same article.'

Without any sense of shame, she had copied my method and printed something herself. She began to read aloud:

'*But now those surprising conclusions have drawn heated criticism from other scientists who claim that the studies' methodology was flawed and the original data completely inadequate to estimate the role that contagion might play in the spread of these behaviours.*'

'I wouldn't pay that much heed,' I said. 'The point is Christakis and Fowler are firm about their conclusions. Scientists are always sceptical about other scientists' work—that's the way the game is played in technical circles.'

'And of course, you're an expert on scientific matters,' she said.

I smiled modestly.

'I was being sarcastic,' she said. 'In any case, even if there is some truth in this, I can't go around convincing your friends to lose weight and wait for the ripples to reach you, and you miraculously start shedding kilograms. I'm sorry, it's still more exercise and less eating for you.'

As usual, when faced with overwhelming evidence, she dug in her heels and stuck to her archaic viewpoint. I wondered if she too was so stubborn because of her friends.

The stranger danger

I WAS TRAVELLING WITH MY COLLEAGUE Faisal Khan for a presentation to a client in Bangkok. We were idling away the half-hour before the flight browsing at the bookshop at Singapore's Changi airport when a bespectacled balding man walked up to us and gave Faisal a nice thump on his shoulder.

'Faisal!' he cried. 'How nice to see you after so long!'

I could see that Faisal was flustered. He shook the man's hand and in a shaking voice said, 'Sorry, do I know you?'

'Know me!? By God man, we studied at school together.'

'Oh, sorry, is it Alok Nagpal?' asked Faisal.

'No! Of course not!' The man was obviously hurt to be mistaken for Nagpal.

'Sorry,' said Faisal apologetically. 'It's Ronnie Fernandes, right?' The man shook his head, looking even more sorrowful. 'Ramesh Manduskar?' As Faisal threw this last name, I could see he was merely shooting in the dark.

'No man! I'm Jaya. D. Jayachandran.'

Faisal apologized nicely and the two friends talked for a while, till it was time to board our flight.

As I sat down next to Faisal, I said to him: 'That was a miserable performance at the bookshop.'

'I know,' he said. 'I can remember people's names but I can't remember their faces, especially when they change so much with time. I just can't get my memory to perform.'

'I'm not talking about your memory,' I said sternly. 'I'm talking about your performance in handling the situation. Let me tell you something: my memory is worse than yours. You claim you remember names but not the face that goes with it and I have friends who swear their problem is the reverse. My memory shows neither bias—I usually forget both face and name. And like it happened to you today, I often meet 'strangers' at airports who know me. Over the years, I've developed some simple, yet cunning, tactics to cope with this hazard. Today I'm going to pass these on to you so you don't make the bloomers you made with Jayachandran today.

'My ordeal usually starts with a cry of "Hi Jags" followed by a stranger approaching with hand extended and a silly grin plastered on his face.

'I don't grasp the hand straight away. No, first I subtly stumble and drop something to create an opportunity, while we're bending down, to *Look for His Name on His Luggage*. I'm at my best if I have a cup of coffee (or tea—both work equally well) in my hand. With a smooth movement of the hand (akin to what I employ for my backhand volley), I knock the cup against the extended hand of aforementioned stranger, spilling liquid here and there. While he fumbles around in guilt, looking for handkerchiefs and so on, I closely examine his luggage.'

'What if he doesn't tag his luggage?' asked Faisal.

'Many don't,' I said. 'In that case I shake his hand with energy, and say: 'Hi! How have you been? Tell me in detail.'

'I then *Simply Wait for Him to Reveal His Name while Talking about Himself*. People usually talk about themselves unprompted, as you may have noticed. When actually *requested* to do so, they blossom. I listen, hoping for something like this:

'"As I scored my third birdie, my opponent said, 'Anand, you give me an inferiority complex.'"

'Or: "When I repaired the sink before my wife could call the plumber, she said, 'Rajeev, what would I do without you?'"

'I then chip in at the next break and say: "Anand or Rajeev, it's fascinating to know what you've been up to..."'

'What if they don't talk about themselves?' Faisal wanted to know.

'They always do. But they don't always speak out their own name. So another technique I employ is simple but effective: I *Exchange Business Cards*.

'"We must stay in touch," I say, '"Do you have a card? Here's mine."'

'I've tried that!' cried Faisal. 'But many idiots don't carry their business cards with them.'

'You're right,' I said. 'In that case I have to resort to a more devious device—I *Ask for His Boarding Pass*. "Show me your boarding pass, I say. Let me see if your seat is close to mine."'

'Does this work?' Faisal looked doubtful.

'It usually works well,' I said. 'But sometimes the other person acts difficult and says he's on a different flight. I don't let this block me. I say: "I know, but I still like to compare seats. It's a hobby."'

'Sometimes the stranger accosts me before I check in. I then have to *Look at His Other Belongings*.

'"Wow! What a beautiful briefcase!" I say. I pluck it from his hand and search it systematically for ownership details. You may be tempted—because it's easier—to ask for and examine the person's mobile phone but the damn thing rarely carries the owner's name. Once, when the owner was distracted by someone else, I had a few minutes alone with his mobile phone. I called "Home" to find out whose home it was; his wife answered, "Hi Darling!" and was miffed to hear a stranger's voice, that too one who asked who her husband was... the whole thing became rather embarrassing. No, stick to briefcase or handbag.'

'Okay,' said Faisal.

'Another useful technique I employ,' I said, 'is when I have a fellow-traveller with me. I drag them into the conversation and *Perform a Half-Introduction.* You could have done this today by saying: "This is my colleague, Jags Srinivasan" and turned towards me. As I shook hands with him, he would have revealed his name and you would have been listening attentively and taking notes.'

I was pleased to see that Faisal was taking notes now.

'But sometimes,' I said, 'I forget the name of my fellow-traveller. Not you, of course,' I added because he looked a little worried. 'I know who you are. When this happens, I have the opportunity of killing two birds with one stone—I *Perform a Less-than-Half-Introduction.* "I don't believe you both have met," I say and immediately get distracted into doing something else, like receiving an imaginary phone call. (Remember: it is important not to get so distracted that you forget to listen to their introductions because the idea is to emerge from the "phone call" with "Sorry Chris, sorry Sukumar, had to take that call.")

'As you have taken down these notes, memorize them,' I said. 'And you might like to carry a card in your wallet with the key techniques summarized as follows:

- *Look for His Name on His Luggage*
- *Simply Wait and for Him to Reveal Name while Talking about Himself*
- *Exchange Business Cards*
- *Ask for Boarding Pass*
- *Look at Other Belongings* (briefcases and handbags yield best results)
- *Perform a Half-Introduction* if you know the name of your fellow traveller
- *Perform a Less-than-Half-Introduction* if you don't

'So go forth confidently,' I said in closing, 'to any airport to board any flight to any destination, armed with the knowledge that, though there are strangers lurking there to waylay you, you have an array of crafty devices to handle the situation and fly away with reputation intact.'

The after-pitch effect

THE GRONOLLERS PITCH WENT EXTREMELY well. The managing director Bernard Fischhof, a tall bulky Austrian with blond hair and blue eyes, was in a good mood when the meeting started and I thought his geniality rose considerably after he visited the men's room during the coffee break, along with his two lieutenants, the marketing manager and the consumer research manager.

When we reached the end of our presentation, Fischhof was beaming.

'I have a few questions, as I'm sure my colleagues do too. But why don't we go out for lunch somewhere and talk?'

Chris Skinner and I exchanged a grin. Nothing indicates that a client is happy with the agency like an impromptu invitation to lunch (unless the meeting gets over in the evening and it's an invitation to a drink).

'Good idea, Bernard,' said Nitin Pandey, Gronollers' marketing director. 'But let me visit the loo first. Rather do it here than at the restaurant. Can never be sure of the quality of the soap there, right?'

'Right!' said Fischhof. 'And the toilet paper! Ha, ha, ha!'

As the three Gronollers executives laughed happily, Skinner gave me a subtle thumbs-up sign, which I acknowledged with a modest smile. After all, it had been my suggestion to change the soap and toilet paper in the bathrooms to Gronollers' brands.

At lunch I sat on one side of Fischhof and Skinner on the other. We chatted amicably about Gronollers, the advertising industry, life in general and the specific food we were eating. A spirit of genial bonhomie reigned.

'You guys really understand Gronollers,' said Fischhof. Then he turned to look at me with his piercing blue yes. 'But Jags, you in particular seem to get our pulse particularly well!'

'I did my summer internship at Gronollers,' I said. I began to fondly talk about my stint with Ashutosh Ojha, that intense brand manager of Swipe. I could still recall things as if they had happened a few weeks ago instead of several years.

'Those were happy days,' I said. 'Do you know Ojha?'

'Yes!' said Fischhof. 'When I was in Brazil several years ago, he and I were on the global Operation Lightning Rod project.'

'Operation Lightning Rod!?' I was excited to hear the term again.

During my summer internship at Gronollers, I had helped Ojha with some analysis on this project, whose objective was to win the laundry war in developing markets by getting India, Brazil, and China to work together. It had been given a code name, standard Gronollers practice initiated by a former CEO who was ex-military. Gronollers executives take pains to select the code name. Ojha had proudly told me that he had put forth the name 'Operation Lightning Rod' to contend with 17 others; it had won after three rounds of voting.

Fischhof and I discussed Operation Lightning Rod with fond nostalgia. We talked about the exciting comparisons we had drawn between three countries: the washing habits of rural women; the popular pack sizes of laundry versus cooking oil and rice; the propensity to wear white versus coloured clothes; and the cooking method used and its impact on soiling clothes (for example: is the dirt caused by cooking in the chulha—earthen oven—dirtier than that induced by an open grill?).

'What became of the project?' I asked after five minutes of happy reminiscing.

'When Gronollers exited the laundry business in Brazil,' said Fischhof, 'interest waned... then disappeared.'

'Oh well, fun always comes to an end,' I said philosophically.

'Tell me, Jags,' Fischhof leaned forward and subjected me to another penetrating gaze of his deep blue eyes. 'Would you like to work in Gronollers again?'

'Yes!' It was true. The last month's preparation for the Gronollers pitch, topped up with this conversation over lunch, had ignited my original passion.

He invited me for another lunch later that week, after which he arranged interviews with three more Gronollers executives over the next month. The result was an offer to join Gronollers as a marketing director of their laundry category. During the same period, Gronollers had confirmed Q&P as the RTD advertising agency for their Jolly Juice range. When I told Skinner about my decision to join Gronollers, he grinned.

'I could see something was cooking over lunch the other day,' he said. 'While I'm sorry to see you go, it'll be nice to have an inside man at Gronollers!'

Devious inanimate objects

Soon I joined the Gronollers ship and began sailing familiar marketing waters. Life settled into a routine, which of course included attending the odd party. In one such get-together I was chatting with R. Sambasivan, an old friend from college also working in Singapore.

'Ah! Things, glorious things! They do the work for us and make life so comfortable,' gushed Sambasivan.

'On the contrary, they make life difficult,' I said.

Sambasivan was shocked and asked me to explain myself. I was happy to do this as I had spent some time analyzing the topic.

'There are two techniques inanimate objects use to befuddle man,' I said. '(A) not working and (B) getting lost.'

'What do you mean?' Sambasivan said. 'Don't talk theory, man! Give me some examples.'

I proceeded to do so. In the first category, I explained, are things like my home printer, electric shaver and coffee maker, which frustrate by *not working*.

'The other day,' I said, 'when I instructed my home printer to print something, it promptly instructed *me* to check (one by one) the *cartridge*, the *paper tray* and the *print settings*. After I did this, it started printing with the sound of a small aircraft taking off... only to stop midway and tell me to *clear the paper jam*. Easier said than done. I had to do it forcefully because the printer maintained a vice-like grip on the paper and gently to avoid damaging the paper. The paper tore in my hand. I had to remove it shred by painful shred, using my fingernails and my wife's tweezers (without telling her). In the end, I simply took pen and paper and copied what was on the computer screen by hand.'

Sambasivan was nodding sympathetically. Obviously he owned a home printer too.

'The second example,' I said, 'is my electric shaver. It too does not work properly, but employs a different method to do it. Its motor rotates and its blades vibrate, but it doesn't shave. Before buying it, I had watched the same model on television, imparting a silky smooth shave to a famous macho sportsman with stubble like a wire brush. The next day, when I emerged from the bathroom after using it, my wife asked me why I had not shaved. I've not used the gadget since then.'

'And the third example,' I continued, 'is my coffee machine. My printer and electric shave don't work properly, but my coffee machine doesn't work at all. I remember proudly bringing it home after watching a salesgirl demonstrate its use at the mall. The first brewing was not a spectacular success. I used too much coffee and did not screw on the filter holder tightly: so hot water—along with granules of coffee—began to leak out of the sides. By the time I salvaged the wreck and extracted some coffee, it was lukewarm and weak. But soon I got the hang of the machine and began to use it regularly. A week ago, with no provocation, it stopped working. Applying the technical knowledge I had imbibed at engineering school, I switched it off and on and tapped it sharply but it refused to budge. When I called the help desk, the woman happily told me that the product was no longer under warranty and quoted an astronomical figure for repairing it. "But it makes more sense to buy a new machine than repair it," I said. She agreed with me and invited me to come and look at the models they have.'

'I don't have a coffee machine,' said Sambasivan. 'Maybe I shouldn't buy one.'

'Absolutely not. Now let me tell you about the second category. These are objects that find it difficult to *work poorly* or *not work* at all. I'm talking about things like keys, spectacles, pens, scissors, scotch tape, staplers, post-it notes, nail cutters, USB sticks and the funny contraptions storing electronic codes to access bank accounts. Therefore they *get lost*. My car keys are particularly good at this. When I'm in the office, they get out of my briefcase and park themselves in my desk drawer or computer bag, or travel to the pantry or conference room. At home, they have been known to leave the side table in the living room, travel across the dining room, pass through the kitchen, open the heavy back door, clamber up my top-loading washing machine, open the lid, rummage among the clothes till they find my trousers, maneuver themselves into the pockets and sit there smirking while I ransack the house searching.'

'You're so right!' said Sambasivan. 'Now that I think of it, I realize that, between my car and its keys, they give me hell. The car keeps breaking down; when it works, the keys keep getting lost. And now I think the car is learning from the keys. Last Sunday, it got lost in the mall's multi-story parking lot.'

'But the most diabolical inanimate object is the television remote control,' I told Sambasivan. 'Because it can *get lost* as ingeniously as car keys and *not work* as efficiently as a coffee maker. My TV remote freely travels from living room to bedroom, bathroom, balcony, kitchen, and sometimes even the car outside. The other day, after spending an hour looking for it—and missing a nail-biting reality show—I got a headache and went to the refrigerator for ice. And there, nestled next to the ice tray, I found the TV remote. But it simply would not work. It had gone and frozen itself to death. I tried warming it in the microwave but it wouldn't budge. In the end I had to replace it.'

Sambasivan nodded thoughtfully.

'Mull that over,' I said. 'I'm getting myself another drink and saying hi to Basu. I see he has just walked in.'

Fridge, oh glorious fridge

TEN MINUTES LATER, HAVING ACQUIRED a drink and met with Basu, I noticed Sambasivan was still sitting in the same place, deep in thought. I walked over.

'Jags,' he said. 'You've opened my eyes! Oh, these cursed inanimate objects!'

'There, there,' I said and patted him on this back. 'I didn't mean to depress you. It's not that bad.'

'It's worse,' he said. 'My car keys, I realize, are worse blackguards than you describe. They can not only get lost, they can also not work.'

'How can keys not work, Samba?' I said. 'You must have tried them on the wrong car. I've done that sometimes.'

'No! It was my car. I know because it was in my porch, where no other cars can be parked. But when I approached it ten minutes before an important appointment and pushed the remote, nothing happened. The remote battery had died. So of course I tried to open the car manually. That's when I realized for the first time—though I've had the car for a year—that the plastic thingummy, a centimeter thick, could never fit in the thin keyhole. I might as well have tried to insert my finger. In fact,' he said, looking around to ensure no one else could hear him, 'in my desperation, I actually tried to insert my finger. I had to call the dealer—

he explained how to open the plastic remote and find the metal key inside, hidden beautifully. By the time I opened the car, I was already ten minutes late for my meeting.'

I commiserated with him but he seemed inconsolable.

'You've made me realize how frustrated I am with all these wretched things in my life,' he said. I felt guilty because this was the same man who had opened the evening's conversation with a eulogy of inanimate objects.

'I have half a mind to give it all up and retire in some cave yonder.' He pointed vaguely in the northern direction.

'Hang on, hang on,' I said. I had to restore the man's equanimity. 'All inanimate objects are not bad. Let me tell you about one inanimate object that makes our living worthwhile.' A glimmer of hope came into his sad eyes. 'The refrigerator. What a glorious machine! I've always had one at home. What about you?'

'Me too,' he said softly.

'Well,' I continued. 'Every morning I find it in the same corner I left it the previous night, humming away in its characteristic unobtrusive manner. It has never got lost. Has yours?'

He shook his head.

'And in all these years,' I said, 'my fridge has never stopped working. We've banged into it, left its door carelessly open for hours and crammed its interior with all sorts of food we need and much that we don't. But it never complains, never takes a day off, and never shuts down. Even during power cuts in India, while we used to fret and fume, it would maintain its cool, so to speak, for hours.'

Sambasivan buoyed up considerably. 'You're right, Jags. My fridge has always been there for me, reliable and steadfast. How could I forget it? Next time I feel despondent about my other wretched things, I will think about the wonderful fridge and calm myself. Thank you, my friend. You've shown me the way.'

He ambled off to meet other people in a state of peace, his faith in inanimate objects, and therefore life, at least partly restored. But my eloquent words had stirred my own emotions about my steadfast, staunch, and true refrigerator.

Of course, with other inanimate objects slacking off by not working or losing themselves, it was easy to get impressed by a machine that simply stays put and works, just as it is easy to applaud the government employee who arrives for work before everyone else at 11 am and doesn't take his first tea-break till 11.45. But the refrigerator was truly worthy of adulation because of the noble duty it performed: storing food and providing it upon request. I approached it the first thing every morning to get milk for my tea, the last thing every night for a late-night snack to keep me going while sleeping, and several times in between for refreshments.

My wife also provided food but in a very different manner. For example, just the previous day, she had entered the house with shopping bags and I had immediately sniffed chocolate cake. I asked her to give me that particular packet. Instead, she gave me my cholesterol score and after dinner, cut me a piece of cake the size of a cashew nut.

I contrasted her behaviour with the refrigerator's when I approached it after Vidya went to sleep. Without making any telltale squeaks, it had allowed me to open its door silently and released the cake without a murmur. When I had cut a proper piece, it had not made clucking noises. And when I had returned the considerably diminished cake, it had not sarcastically asked me if I've had enough.

Before hitting the bed that night, I idly browsed through Roland Berger Strategy Consultants' prediction about the future home. As I read it, I began to fear for my blissful life with my refrigerator. The report said:

'When entering your home in 2030, discreet computerized agents sense your needs, monitor your environment, and await your spoken instructions. All electronic devices are connected, e.g. a message will appear on the wallpaper while you are watching your favorite 5D movie to tell you that your meal is ready.'

My God! I imagined myself in this hi-tech house approaching the refrigerator when my wife is away and finding it locked. I then imagined an eerie conversation taking place between the machine and me.

'Open up!' I order.

'Why?' it asks.

'I want pistachio ice-cream.'

'Ooh!' It draws in its breath sharply. 'One scoop is 435 calories. Your weight is...'

'Never mind that. Open up.'

'Sorry, no can do. I'm programmed to open only after you burn 550 calories in the gym, which the computer there will tell me. We're connected,' it adds smugly.

'Oh, are you?' I ask in a menacing tone, 'And who programmed you?'

'The Boss.'

I realize this is my wife and quickly change from menacing to beseeching tone.

'Oh. Please don't tell her about this conversation.'

'Too late—it's being emailed to her even as we speak.'

The EE's and SS's of marketing at Gronollers

'Swipe is Gronollers' premium detergent brand and the pride of the company,' I told the three marketing trainees who had joined Gronollers recently. 'In your visit to R&D, you would have learnt about Zyphillon X, the proprietary cleaning technology in Swipe. Five years ago, R&D trademarked Zyphy Lite, a diluted version of Zyphillon X that delivers 80 percent of its cleaning effect and we launched the Cheetah brand to compete at the lower end of the detergent market.'

'For poor people?' asked Sarah Barker, the petite trainee from Australia.

'No, for smart people!' I said. 'We don't refer to our consumers as poor (even if they are). Cheetah appeals to Savvy Superiority (SS in short). Like Walmart.'

'And Ikea?' suggested Abhishek Sharma, the management grad from India. 'Their slogan is: *You don't have to be rich to be clever.*'

'Exactly!' I said. 'Many Gronollers brands cater to SS. At the other end brands cater to Expensiveness Ego (or EE). EE makes people pay premium prices for brands so others know they have done so. A Rolex watch, for example, does not tell time better than a Casio but what it does tell much better is that the person wearing it is rich. Name the Gronollers brand catering to EE.'

'PL7?' ventured the third trainee from Singapore, Peter Tan.

'Excellent!' I said. 'PL7 is Gronollers premium beauty brand with a range of creams and facial products. Nothing is priced below US$ 100.'

'But people don't wear their tube of face cream on their wrist like a watch,' objected Sharma.

'They don't need to,' I said. 'They mention it casually, as in: "When I reached the hotel in Amsterdam, I panicked. I had forgotten to bring my PL7, which I use twice a day. Luckily the concierge was able to help me get some." PL7 also runs spas in Singapore and other major cities, where people meet and indulge in a mutual EE experience.'

'So, wealthy people exhibit EE and poor people—sorry, I mean smart people—exhibit SS?' asked Barker.

'Not always. The woman in a BMW car may relish saving $14 on strawberries and the man in Armani may have bought the suit by extending his credit card to dangerous limits.'

'Let's get back to the laundry subject,' I continued, nodding to Barker. 'As I was saying, Cheetah addresses SS. Its slogan is: *Washes your clothes AND watches your wallet*.'

'And does Swipe address EE?' asked Barker.

She had touched a raw nerve. 'Not yet. It's an issue with the whole detergent category. Though we've featured celebrities like the oil tycoon Anna Silversmith using Swipe, we can't get women to talk about their detergent the way they do about their handbag. Men are worse. I've watched men spend 45 minutes discussing cars but the moment I introduce laundry into the topic, they tune off.'

'That's not fair!' said Tan. 'In many ways laundry is more useful than a mere car.'

'You take the words out of my mouth!' I said. 'Can you wear a clean car on your first date to impress your girlfriend?'

'And can you surprise your husband by removing a barbeque stain from his favourite car and placing it in his cupboard for him to discover when he next opens it?' said Barker.

'Exactly!' I said. 'Our challenge is to make Swipe as EE a brand as Cheetah is an SS one. You can't mix EE and SS.'

Funnily enough, that very evening, when I met an old school friend at the pub, I discovered that you can... sometimes.

'Let's order two drinks each quickly,' I said as he leisurely read through the menu. 'Happy Hour closes in four minutes.'

He looked at his watch with a flamboyance that demanded I look, too.

'Wow! A Rolex!' I said.

'It's nothing,' he said modestly, 'I have another one that's even better.'

Then he leaned forward, looked into my eyes and dropped his voice.

'They're both fake,' he said, 'I paid $500 for both in Kuala Lumpur. Look at the craftsmanship! Can you make out the difference? Two real Rolexes would've cost me $15,000? Smart, huh?'

'Very smart,' I said, 'and savvy. But I'm puzzled. Why buy a fake Rolex and *advertise* it's fake? Surely that defeats the whole purpose?'

'Laundry is more useful than a mere car. Can you wear a clean car on your first date to impress your girlfriend?'

'Oh, no!' he said. 'I tell everyone it's a real Rolex. Except my wife. If I'd told her it's real, she'd have insisted on buying a genuine Prada. But other than her, I've only told you. Want to know why?'

I nodded eagerly. I was touched that he considered me so close.

'Noticing your vigilance about Happy Hour,' he said, 'I realized you would be more impressed that I'd saved thousands of dollars buying a fake Rolex than thinking I had a real one.' He slapped me on my back. 'You are still the same penny-counting cheapskate you were in college.'

Supermarket man

'OH NO!' MY WIFE GROANED. 'We've run out of cooking oil and there's very little rice. There's too much food consumption in this house!' She looked at me pointedly.

'Okay, I'll go to the supermarket,' I said, cleverly choosing to interpret her glare as cry-for-help instead of accusation. 'Give me a list.'

I approach grocery shopping in much the same way as Usain Bolt approaches the 100-metre sprint: with keenness, tenacity and an unwavering will to win. When my wife gave me the list, written in her usual haphazard fashion, I rewrote it in the order of the way things are arranged in the supermarket's aisles so I would not waste time going back and forth. As Mr Bolt will tell you, the 100-metres is a straight race: you don't meander your way through it. As I redid the list, I added items like cake, crisps, and cookies that are very necessary for sustenance but, as usual, my wife had left out.

At the supermarket, I tested three trolleys before picking the smoothest, in the same way as Mr Bolt tries different shoes before making his selection for the race. I then made my efficient way through the store, picking up items and immediately making a corresponding tick on the list. In this respect, I even out-did Mr Bolt: I've never seen him carrying a list and putting a tick against each opponent's name as he streaks past them.

At the 'Snacks' section, I was delighted to discover my favourite brand of roasted peanuts. I picked it up though it was not on my list (I had not included it because it had been out of stock for three months). I mention this only to illustrate my spontaneity and on-the-spot decisiveness. I believe Mr Bolt, based on wind and track conditions, makes similar on-the-spot adjustments to his running strategy on the day of the race. But to ensure everything was methodical and above-board, I wrote down 'Roasted peanuts' in my list and put a neat tick against it.

As I reached the ice-cream refrigerator I saw that there was exactly one tub left of 'Nestle Crunch' (featured prominently on my list). Congratulating myself, I carefully ticked the item on my list, opened the door of the fridge and reached inside...

'Got the last tub, mom!' A roly-poly boy had grabbed the ice cream just before my fingers could touch it. I gave him a cold, nasty look but his back was already turned to me as he ran back to his mother, who was wheeling a trolley away from us. Shaking my head at the Insolence of Youth, I went back to the refrigerator and after careful deliberation, decided on 'Meadowgold Cookies and Cream' as my second choice. I was sorely disappointed but I bore it philosophically, telling myself that on another day, I would win the 'Nestle Crunch' race. Usain Bolt would probably console himself in the same way if he ever ends up second in a sprint.

By the time I reached my car, the ice cream debacle was forgotten. As I lined up the boot with my packages, I felt a warm glow of something-attempted-something-done, similar to what Mr Bolt feels every time he cuts the finish-line tape. Then a chill intruded the warm glow as I thought about taking the things into my home. I had augmented my wife's list with items that promised gastronomic pleasure in the near future, but I knew from experience that she would (a) not share my joy at these purchases and, instead of keeping her feelings bottled up, (b) express her lack-of-joy unequivocally. I realized that, just like Mr Bolt, who finishes the 100-metre sprint and gets ready for the 200-metre event a little later, I had another race to run.

It would be easy if my wife had gone for a walk when I entered so I could unpack and store the things on my own. Then I shook myself and thought: that's a cowardly attitude, not befitting a sportsman. Would Usain Bolt hope all his opponents get a false start, leaving him alone to run the race? So I squared my shoulders and began to warm up mentally for the upcoming encounter.

Close encounters of the durian kind

I HAD BEEN IN SINGAPORE FOR a few years when my colleague David Tan asked me if I'd tried the durian.

'No,' I said. 'By which I mean, not yet. I'm always in the market for trying something new to eat. Tell me about the durian.'

'It's the king of fruits,' he replied enthusiastically. 'Do you like custard?'

'Yes.'

'And almonds?'

'Yes.' It was an understatement: I loved almonds.

'Then you have to like the durian: it's a combination of the two.'

Excited, I promised to try it. At a local fruit market a few days later, I saw (and smelt) durians sitting on a special table with a dedicated salesman. He did not need to market the fruits. They were selling briskly on their own: he was merely collecting the cash. I bought a fruit, took it home, laid it on the coffee table in the living room and, brandishing a knife, invited the family to a feast.

I have to say that the feast was not a success. The next day I told Tan I had tried the durian.

'And...?' he asked eagerly.

'Firstly, I messed up our sofa while cutting it.'

'You always place the durian on layers of newspapers before cutting it,' he said. It was illuminating advice... delivered one day late.

'Secondly, I couldn't eat it,' I said. 'The smell was strong, the taste even stronger. When you said it tastes like custard and almonds, are you sure you meant the durian, and not some almond-flavoured custard you had recently eaten?'

'No!' he said, 'I was referring to the durian. And I did not make up that description. I was quoting Alfred Russel Wallace, the 19th century naturalist.'

He was right, I discovered that evening on Google. Wallace had had a special affection for the durian, describing it eloquently: *'A rich custard highly flavoured with almonds... It is neither acid nor sweet nor juicy... it is in itself perfect... the more you eat of it the less you feel inclined to stop.'* And Wallace was a naturalist of repute: it was his theory of evolution that had inspired Charles Darwin to publish his treatise about natural selection. If a man of this stature was so gung-ho about the durian, I had to cultivate a taste for it.

It was also a matter of pride. I was disconcerted to find something difficult to eat. It happened rarely, as my wife often says. If it's edible (and had not breathed previously), chances are I would like it.

But after that first encounter with the durian, I felt reluctant to try again. What if I could induce a friend to try it with me? I approached Ravi Bhaskaran.

'The durian,' I told him, 'is South East Asia's king of fruit. The origin of the name, *duri*, means...'

'Huge distance!' He interrupted me. 'I always keep my *duri* from it.' As he laughed, I got the distinct feeling he had been carrying that joke in his back-pocket, waiting to unload it on someone. When I asked him to accompany me on my durian adventure, he laughed louder. 'I've tried it once,' he said. 'Never again.'

A couple of days later at the office, I was having lunch, which I had brought from home, when David Tan—the man who had urged me try the durian—walked over.

'Jags, have you acquired a taste for the durian?'

'Not yet,' I replied. 'It's very strong, you know. And the taste is very strange.'

'What's that you're eating now?' he asked.

'My lunch—try some?'

'What's in this box?' He pointed to the first container. I explained that it was *upma* and described it. He took a spoonful into his mouth and grimaced.

'But it's sweet!' he said. 'And I can taste banana in it.'

'Yes, we habitually mash a ripe banana into the *upma*, add some sugar and make a blend of the whole thing. Have some more.'

'It's an interesting taste,' he said politely, 'But no thanks. And what's this other stuff in the second box?'

'Curd-rice,' I said, 'Rice and yoghurt mixed together nicely with a sprinkle of salt.'

'What are those yellow things in it?'

'Good question!' I said, 'It's the mango season and the Banganapalli—a great variety of the fruit from Tamil Nadu—is available in Singapore.'

'You mean you've cut pieces of this Banganapalli mango and added it to the rice?'

'Yes.' I could not understand his astonishment. 'But I'm not wedded to the Banganapalli—sometimes I add Aphonso too. Here, try a spoonful.'

He declined gracefully.

'Tell me one thing,' he said. 'If you can eat such exotic combinations, how can you find the taste of the durian strange?'

Laundry Immersion Day

I RETURNED HOME AT 8 PM after a three-day trip, bursting with the desire to tell Vidya about it. However, I've known her to resist my attempts to talk about my marketing manoeuvres when she is in the middle of something and she was watching television now. I needed to introduce the topic subtly so that she did not feel I was 'thrusting the detergent topic down my throat again'.

As the ads started, I got ready to speak when she gave me the perfect cue by laughing at the end of a commercial and saying, 'That was funny… I wonder how they come up with ideas like that.'

'Ah!' I said quickly. 'Let me explain Laundry Immersion Day, a new process we started at Gronollers. I'm just returning from the session.'

'No, no, don't bother!' she said. 'It was a rhetoric question.'

'Not a bother at all,' I said, casually picking up the remote and switching off the television set as I sat down next to her.

'But *Casual Acquaintances* is about to start,' she protested.

'You can catch the rerun tomorrow,' I said and began: 'Laundry Immersion Day started with muffins and coffee,' I said, 'enough to give us energy without dulling our faculties. From 9 am till lunch, we discussed how economic factors like the wholesale price index, crude oil imports, and education enrolment were impacting the average household and therefore affecting the sales of Swipe, Cheetah, and their competitors.'

'Ah, I get it,' said Vidya, when I paused briefly—merely to take a breath, which I had forgotten to do while talking—'The agency heard all this and made the ad.' She tried to reach for the TV remote but I had cleverly put it in my pocket.

'No!' I said, 'The agency's role was to absorb. The planning and account people were doing this well but I caught the creative director sleeping when we were discussing inflation curves of South Africa and Indonesia. You can be sure he got it from me severely for that.'

'After lunch,' I continued, 'the agency took us through the advertising on Swipe and Cheetah for the last two years: once normally, then without sound to gauge the visual impact and a third time on fast forward to see if the story was still clear.'

'Okay, *then* the agency made the ad,' said Vidya.

'No! It was Immersion Day—we only immersed ourselves in knowledge. Next we observed consumer behaviour: we watched them wash their clothes.'

'What?! In the conference room?!'

'No, we went to their homes, one by one, observed them for three hours and summarized our findings for an hour. After dinner, we attended three focus group discussions for an hour each: among middle-aged housewives, young working women and married men. At 10 pm we did a quick recap and retired to our hotel.'

'Very nice explanation of Immersion Day,' said Vidya, 'Thanks.'

'It's not over,' I said coldly.

'You retired to the hotel.'

'For that day only,' I said. 'Laundry Immersion Day lasted three days. But if we called it anything else, like 'Laundry Immersion Week', it would've sounded daunting.'

'I wonder why,' said my wife. 'But, while I don't mind missing *Casual Acquaintances*, I have to catch the BBC news. Give me the remote now. We can continue this conversation later.'

I began to protest but seeing the look on her face, stopped.

'Okay, I'll continue tomorrow,' I said. 'Or the day after,' I added hastily seeing that her look had hardened.

Helping out with homework

'APPA, I NEED SOME HELP with my homework,' my daughter Preeti said. 'How does kinetic energy change to potential energy in a spring?'

When my children were young, helping them with their homework was a satisfying task that would leave me feeling warm and fuzzy, like a freshly baked muffin. I had started by helping Preeti add 14 and 22. She had looked at me with wonder in her little eyes. Then I had shown my son Anand the location of the North Pole on the globe and he had clapped his tiny hands in delight. Next I'd explained the difference between feet and metres—conceptually of course (only the mobile phone knows the actual conversion factors nowadays) and my children had nodded with mouths open. I got into a problem-solving stride, sitting with my children on many evenings, sorting out their problems. As a habitual homework helper, I gained the respect of my children (they would say to Vidya: 'Dad knows stuff!') as well as their teachers, who, I discovered, love people to share their workload but not their salary.

What I hadn't realized was that sooner or later, as I walked on the velvet grass of problem-solving, I would step on a pitchfork and the question-I-had-no-clue-about would hit me square between the eyes. That's what happened now.

I could have said, 'I don't know' and moved on but this may have stopped her and her brother endearingly saying, 'Dad knows stuff.'

Suddenly I got a flash of brilliance.

'Let me tell you about energy,' I said. 'The more energy you use by exercising, the healthier you become. At your age, I used to get up at 6 am daily and go for a run.' I said this with solemn reproach even though, as a child, I did not get up, in the strictest sense of the word, at exactly 6 am. 'Before I help with this question, please go for a brisk ten-minute run and return. Quick—off you go!' When she was away I attacked the computer with gusto.

A few days later, my son asked me: 'What's the capital of Italy?'

I said: 'Did you know that in Italy, children run an average fourteen kilometres every week, making them the planet's fittest kids? Before I answer the question, go for a brisk ten-minute run and return. Quick—off you go!'

I realized I had stumbled on a great method. Apart from the obvious benefit of preventing me from looking dumb, it discouraged future homework consultations. Having an MBA bent of mind, I chronicled the method so that I could perfect it and offer it to other parents to use correctly.

Like any management technique, it needed a catchy name, so I called it the 3Ds of Dealing with Homework Requests: Delay, Discomfort, Dig Deep. When your child asks a difficult homework question, use the question as a guide to provide advice (Delay) that requires your child to take some unsavoury action (Discomfort); while your child is engaged, Google the answer (Dig Deep) and be ready.

As I practised the 3Ds technique, I realized that, while making the children go for a run was an excellent way to cause Delay and Discomfort, it wasn't practical to do it *always*, for example at night or if my child were feeling unwell. I found another failsafe option: something I could tell any child during any weather at any time of day: *Tidy Your Room.*

When Preeti asked me why fish have gills, I said: 'Fish are the tidiest creatures on earth...'—whether this was true was irrelevant—'... to learn from. Your room resembles a pig sty. Please go and clean it now.'

When Anand asked how dew forms on the earth, I said: 'Dew has been around on earth before man built neat houses on the grass. But as he had children, they started making the houses messy. Your room resembles a pig sty. Please go and clean it now.'

When I got an abstract question on algebra, I made my answer abstract too: 'Doing algebra requires a tidy mind. A tidy mind cannot happen with an untidy room. Your room resembles a pig sty. Please go and clean it now.'

I can now vouch for this method. So go forth and practise the 3Ds. Google while your child goes for a run or tidies their room. If you do it a few times, all requests for help with homework—even if they concern geography—will be history for you.

Mobile love

I USED TO THINK THAT THE disease caused by mobile phones was addiction. But after reading an article by Martin Lindstrom in *The New York Times* recently, I realize the disease is much worse: it is love.

Mr Lindstorm, along with MindSign Neuromarketing, subjected eight men and women to complicated fMRI experiments—which, suffice to say, sounded like complex stuff—and found a frenzied level of activation in the insular cortex of the brain, associated with feelings of love and compassion. In other words, these subjects responded to the sound and vibration of their mobile phones in much the same way as we respond to an affectionately loved one. They actually 'heard' their mobile phones even when it was only vibrating and 'saw' it when it was only ringing. This is similar to looking at your one-year old baby's picture and 'hearing' her prattle, or passing a big log of wood in the park, and 'seeing' your husband snoring next to you at night. And when deprived of their beloved instrument, they exhibited the same anxiety a mother displays when she can't locate her child in the supermarket.

The article must have made a deep impression on me because I had a vivid dream that night.

My colleague Joe Tibault was looking very distressed as he searched his desk, lifting papers and ransacking drawers.

'What happened, Joe?' I asked with concern, 'You're looking ashen and pale.'

'My presentation to management is beginning in 15 minutes,' he said, 'And I can't find...'

'... your presentation!?' I cried, 'This is terrible! Was it on a USB stick? Don't you have a copy on your computer?'

'Of course I have a copy of my presentation,' said Tibault, 'It's my cell phone I can't find.'

I was puzzled. 'Why do you need your phone? Surely, you can't play Solitaire when you're actually presenting?'

'I never play Solitaire with Sheila!' he snapped, 'That's rude.' Then his face took on a wistful look. 'But we do play Scrabble together sometimes... she's really good, you know.'

My mind began to churn. I knew his wife Helen. Who was Sheila and did Helen know?

'Sheila! Where are you?' he cried in anguish, throwing the papers from his drawer to the floor.

Then I got it: the goof was referring to his phone.

'Here,' I said, offering him my phone, 'Why don't you call it—I mean her?'

'I've tried. She refuses to answer. I think I left her at my bedside this morning. My God! What must she be thinking? This has NEVER happened before. What do I do?'

'Fetch her during lunch,' I said.

'But I need her now!' he cried, 'I've never made a presentation without her in my pocket. When I'm asked a tough question, I need to feel her vibrations—even when she is still—encouraging me. And when I'm explaining complicated charts, I need to hear her sweet ring tone—'Piano Riff' by the way—telling me I'm doing fine.'

He said it with a straight face, but I cringed in embarrassment and looked around me hastily to ensure others were not overhearing me listening to this drivel.

'Can you please fetch her for me?' Tibault took my hand and looked beseechingly into my eyes. 'You can interrupt the meeting and give it to me. Please? Here, take my car. And here are my house keys. And I'll buy you a drink after work today.'

'But will she come with me?' I asked, 'We've never met.'

The sarcasm backfired.

'Good point!' he said, 'Here, take my photo ID with you. And to be safe, wear my jacket. She always feels comfortable in its pocket.'

'No, no,' I said in panic—his jacket was a deep shade of maroon that I preferred not be seen near, let alone inside—'The ID should be enough.'

'No!' he said, 'Do I know Sheila or do you?'

He took off his jacket and manhandled me into it. As I tried to slink quietly through the office, my phone rang and people looked up. I tried to answer it but it only rang louder and louder. Everyone was staring at me.

That's when I woke up and realized my phone *was* ringing—on my bedside.

It was Joe Tibault, asking for help on his upcoming presentation to senior management.

The power of branding

Sarah Barker, Peter Tan and Abhishek Sharma, the three trainees who had joined the marketing department two years ago, had recently been confirmed as full-time employees. In standard Gronollers practice, each of them had been assigned a mentor "to guide them in their assimilation of the Gronollers philosophy and culture". As an assistant brand manager on Swipe, Barker had naturally been assigned to me and I was now having an FYI session with her.

Let me explain what an FYI session is. A few years ago, HR mooted the idea of 'formal, yet informal' sessions for the young managers to meet their mentors.

Soon after we sat down with our food at the company cafeteria, Barker asked about the 'state of branding today'.

'Branding began with burning a brand name on the skin of cattle to mark ownership,' I said. 'Branding today is similar: it's burning your brand name into the minds of consumers, so that they think about it as often as their spouse (and hopefully, with more affection).'

Barker wanted an example.

'Sports is full of examples,' I said. 'For instance, Barclays Premier League is modern aggressive branding at its best. Barclays uses Liverpool's Steven Gerrard and Manchester

United's Ryan Giggs to spread its brand name through their talented feet.'

'Last night,' said Barker, 'I met a Manchester United football fan from Sri Lanka who had just returned from a holiday in London. He said, "I saw something amazing in London recently." I thought he would refer to the British Museum or Buckingham Palace. Instead he said: "Barclays Bank! It's huge! It's amazing that a football tournament would branch off into banking!"'

'Yes, there is a danger that Barclays brands the League better than it does the bank,' I said. 'But their hope would be that when Barclays enters the Sri Lanka market, your friend, along with the millions of other English football fans in the country, will open an account and transfer his life's savings there.'

'Like football has Barclays Premier League,' I continued, 'golf has the Lexus Cup and tennis has the Sony Ericson Open. More and more tournaments are getting branded and the deals are renegotiated every few years so new brands can join. I was at a pub with a fellow tennis enthusiast recently. He said he was very happy the Queens Club Championship, so steeped in tradition and boring, had been renamed Stella Artois Championship. "I love their beer!" he said, taking a big gulp. I had to break the news that Stella Artois was no longer the sponsor; it was now Aegon, which was unfortunately not a beer, but he could buy their insurance. He promised he would.'

'Is it worth branding a full tournament?' asked Barker.

'I'm not sure. But some brand managers feel they can't have enough! Recently my friend asked me if I was following the BNP Paribas tennis, where the top women were playing for their countries. "It's over," I said, "and it was among men playing for themselves." It turns out both of us were right. The Masters 1000 event I watched and the Federation Cup he referred to are both BNP Paribas events. Last year two Aegon tennis tournaments took place in England *at the same time*!'

'Yes, I've notice tournaments being re-named,' said Barker. 'But what are some other branding approaches?'

'You can brand the team instead of the tournament, like New York Red Bulls in American football and Honda Heat in rugby. You spread you brand name among the team's huge fan base across different tournaments.'

'What about individual sports?' asked Barker. 'People like Roger Federer and Rafael Nadal also have a huge fan base.'

'Good point! The concept has not yet caught on but who knows? Future Wimbledon champions may well be called Henry Carlsberg and Julia Bacardi.'

'Wow!' said Barker. 'That would make for some powerful branding in the future.'

'It would,' I said. 'But you need some exposure to some powerful branding taking place today. I need to take you to watch the Indian Premier League, the latest cricket frenzy. Let's go to a sports bar one evening. I will invite Peter Tan and Abhishek Sharma too.'

Something attempted, something done

From time to time I would remind my children how easy they have it in life compared to me at their age. I'm not sure whether these lectures built their character or not but I still did it because they filled me with warm satisfaction.

So when my daughter planned to join her friends that night to watch the film *127 Hours* and promptly went online to book tickets, I pounced upon the opportunity.

'Three clicks for four tickets,' I said. 'You kids have everything easy. In my youth, buying movie tickets was a serious, strenuous affair as indeed it should be.'

'Oh, you had movies in those days?'

I ignored the impertinence and explained how things worked in the good old days. When a new movie was released, I'd ask her mother if she would like to see it ten days later.

'"Yes!" she would cry, perhaps jumping up and down joyously if the film featured Aamir Khan.'

On Monday, I would grimly tell her to expect me home late: I would be buying the movie tickets after office.

'All the best,' she would say, 'I'll pray for you.'

After work, I would take a detour to the cinema hall and join the long line at Advance Booking. The line moved slow enough to enable people to chat with their neighbour or read a newspaper while waiting. But I would stand vigilant, alert to ward off unscrupulous queue jumpers looking to unobtrusively join a newly-discovered brother in the line ahead of me. Reaching the window, I would address the bored booking clerk clearly and succinctly: 'Saturday evening show; *Qayamat Se Qayamat Tak*; balcony; two tickets; one lady.'

'Why "one lady"?' my daughter interrupted, 'Was he interested in who your companion was?'

I laughed. Few things could have interested the wizened old man less. I had to give him that information so he would allot me the coveted seats next to the aisle. It was considered improper for a woman to sit next to a man she did not know well.

'What if you went with more than one woman?'

'No problem: if I went for a movie with Amma, her cousin and two friends, I would sit furthest from the aisle; then Amma; then her cousin who I knew well; then the school friend I knew slightly; and finally at the aisle seat, the second friend I had not met earlier.'

'Got it,' my daughter said, 'And next time, the last woman could shift one seat to accommodate a new friend of Amma's. But what if a few women went for the movie without any male companion?'

Clarifying that I had never been part of such a group, I explained that the clerk allocated such women next to other women so that you would see entire rows filled with women (and compensating rows devoted to men). Then I described how the clerk would sift through the array of differently-coloured printed ticket books on his table, one for each show on each day, pick the right book, leaf through it till he found two contiguous seat numbers near an aisle, tear them off and give them to me. But often the tickets would be sold out… for the whole weekend. And, since the clerk's table couldn't accommodate more than one week's supply of ticket books, I would have to return home and tell my wife her prayers didn't work.

'So you wouldn't watch the movie?' asked my daughter.

'No! I'd simply repeat the procedure the following Monday.'

My daughter, who had probably never spent more than three and a half minutes at a stretch on any activity, could not grasp the concept of waiting one hour in a line for tickets that may not be available.

'You just booked the tickets for *127 Hours* tonight,' I said, 'Do you feel any elation or sense of accomplishment?' She shook her head.

In our time, with movie tickets in our hand, we returned home like triumphant heroes, welcomed by a jubilant family. The feeling of achievement was especially acute for those of us who did not habitually bring home a glowing report card. We would retire that night recalling Henry Wadsworth Longfellow's lines:

Each morning sees some task begun, each evening sees it close;

Something attempted, something done, has earned a night's repose.

Haircut evolution

'What do you miss about your youth?' a young man asked me at a party in Singapore.

'You mean apart from my youth itself?' I asked. He nodded. 'Well, taking all things into consideration, I would say I miss the haircuts of my youth.'

I explained to him that when I was growing up in India (as a lovable child), I paid just one rupee for a haircut. *Everything* was inexpensive then: for the same one rupee—or a different one—I could have bought a bag of sweets, a pocketful of marbles or four tickets for the local football match… if I had pocket money.

'You don't need pocket money: if you need money for anything, simply ask me,' my father would say with the air of a noble benefactor. And yes, I could always *ask* him for money. But he rarely gave it to me.

Once, our local police team was playing the state's football team in our neighbourhood stadium. My friend and I were keen to go.

'I need two rupees,' I said to my father. 'One for a haircut and another for a football match and peanuts with my friend.'

He gave me only one rupee and suggested I do my homework instead of watching the match and eating peanuts (he frequently imparted impractical advice like this). Since my friend's father was of a similar bent of mind, we had a problem.

'Why don't we cut each other's hair,' my friend suggested, 'and use the money for the match?'

I agreed to go first and sat on the floor while he attacked my hair with gusto and a pair of scissors surreptitiously removed from his kitchen when his mother's back was turned.

'How does it look?' I asked when he finished.

'Great,' he said, suppressing a grin.

'Okay, my turn now.'

'No, no need!' he cried. 'One rupee is enough for the football tickets and peanuts. I'll simply go and get a haircut at the barber.'

It was a nice try, but that rupee belonged to me, not the barber. So I sat him down and snipped his hair happily. When I was done, his head resembled the Botswana bush land—barren expanses interspersed with shrubs.

Postponing facing our fathers' wrath, we wisely went first to the football match, where the sight of our ridiculous haircuts provided additional entertainment for the other spectators.

The other thing I miss about those haircuts of my youth is the free massage they came with. The barber would grasp my recently shorn scalp in two meaty hands and knead it like dough; then bring down the underside of his loosely joined palms sharply on my head, his fingers coming together audibly as they moved across: *click, click, click*. For the finale, he would hold my shoulder in a vice-like grip with one arm around my neck and use the other hand to twist my neck sharply to one side causing it to *creak* in surprise. While on the chair, I was terrified of the neck-twisting (but I never protested because I feared the muscular barber—and his array of sharp knives within easy reach—more). However, once it was done, my neck always felt better... but this could well have been relief that it was still attached to my body.

I realized how much I missed these haircuts when I went for my first haircut in Singapore, along with my eight-year old son. A Chinese barber cut our hair quietly. Without the incessant chatter and the continuous *snip-snip* of scissors cutting empty air, both trademarks of the Indian barber, the silence was eerie. When he finished I braced myself for a tough massage but it never came. He was waiting for me at the cash desk... to give me my next shock.

'$10 for your son's haircut,' he said. My jaw dropped but he was yet to deliver the bigger blow. 'And for your haircut—$16.'

'What?!' I said, 'Why should I pay more? I have less hair than he does.'

'Yes!' he said, 'Very less, Lah. Have to cut carefully. Lots of scalp showing already. See.' He pointed out my bald patches in the front mirror and held up another to introduce me to some at the back of my head that I was not yet acquainted with.

That's when I realized that more than the haircut, I missed the *hair* of my youth.

Branding bliss

I INVITED SARAH BARKER, PETER TAN and Abhishek Sharma, our three youngest assistant brand managers who had joined Gronollers as trainees two years ago, to a sports bar in Singapore so that they could witness branding at its best while watching the Indian Premier League (IPL) on television. We sat down at a table with a commanding view of a large TV screen showing an IPL match and ordered beer.

'Royal Challengers Bangalore is playing Mumbai Indians in this 20-20 format,' explained Sharma. His voice took on a professorial tone. 'Let me explain the game. In this crisp form of cricket, each team is allowed...'

'Forget that.' I interrupted him. 'They don't have four days at their disposal to learn how cricket is played. And it's unlikely they'll ever watch it again.' Sharma's face expressed deep shock and pain. 'Yes, yes, I know,' I said soothingly and patted him on the back. 'It's the mother of all games, a religion in its own right and God's gift to the masses but let's just focus on branding today.' I turned to Barker. 'The Bangalore team is sponsored by Royal Challenger whisky.'

'And the Mumbai team by the Indian government?' she ventured.

'No, no: they can't afford it,' I said, 'which means the name of the Mumbai team is still available for sale.

Now let's watch for more branding examples. And have some beer.'

Soon we were sipping beer, our eyes riveted on the television screen.

'What a shot!' the commentator gushed, 'It's in the air, flying towards the boundary… but there's a fielder there… will he catch it? No! It goes over him. It's a DLF Maximum!'

'Wow!' said Peter Tan. 'DLF has branded the goal! What a branding breakthrough!'

'Actually,' I explained, 'It's not a goal. We used to call it a six when I was young. But you're right—it's a branding breakthrough…'

'It's in the air again!' the commentator screamed, 'The fielder is diving… yes! It's a Karbonn Kamaal catch. Surely this is a Citi Moment of Success for the fielding team.'

'It used to be a simple catch earlier,' I said. 'But the Karbonn mobile brand now owns the catch!'

'And every time a catch is taken, does Citibank benefit by branding the Moment of Success?' asked Barker.

'Yes, but also other moments that the commentators decide are spectacular, like when the batsman scores 100. Or 20. Or 4. Or spots his family in the stands and waves to them. The Citi Moment of Success is flexible and the commentators have been trained to use it often.'

Peter Tan, Sarah Barker and Abhishek Sharma were excited. Their faces were flushed and their eyes shone with an inner light. (In the case of Sharma, this might have been because Sachin Tendulkar was batting.)

'Ok folks,' I said. 'You need to earn your beer. As you watch this IPL match, what ideas can you get for Gronollers?'

'Jags,' said Sharma a few minutes later, 'Karbonn has branded the catch already but what if Gronollers' butter

'It's a DLF Maximum!'

Moonbeam could brand the *bungled* catch as in Moonbeam Butterfingers Miss?'

'Superb!' I said. 'Moonbeam will get more exposure than Karbonn, that's for sure. Any others?'

'Here's one!' said Peter Tan. 'What are those three vertical poles called—behind the fellow holding a flat pole in his hand?'

'Wickets,' said Sharma. 'They are there to…'

'Why don't we brand the wickets,' said Tan, 'with our chocolate brand Three Sticks?'

'I like that,' I said. Three Sticks was a new chocolate brand Gronollers had introduced in Europe and US, a single pack with three bars of chocolate—one plain, one with hazelnuts and one with dry fruits—that was doing very well. 'Yes, that's good. With the right training, we can get the commentator to mention the brand almost continuously: "The batsman has taken his stand in front of Three Sticks, the bowler—right arm over Three Sticks—is ready; he bowls a straight ball towards Three Sticks; the batsman plays a cover drive and runs from Three Sticks to Three Sticks on the other side, while the fielder blocks the ball and throws it, trying to hit Three Sticks before batsman can reach Three Sticks." Good one, Peter!'

The others gave their approval to Tan too.

'But let's get some examples on our laundry brands,' I said. 'Sarah?'

'I know!' she said. 'I notice when Three Sticks get hit by the fellow who throws the ball in the funny, roundabout way—bowler did you call him?—the commentator says he's "clean out". Why don't we brand that with Swipe, as in Swipe Clean Out?'

'I love it!' I said, picking up my beer mug. 'Good job, folks! Let's drink to your suggestions.'

Barker took my advice seriously and drank long and deep. Between sips, she stared at her glass in glazed reverie. Suddenly she thumped the table.

'Taking a page from IPL, why don't we brand the very names of games?' she said. 'Why don't we rename tennis as Swipe? Imagine the branding power when two people, person A—' she pointed at her beer glass and placed my glass near it '—and person B are talking. A asks B: "Do you play Swipe?" B replies: "On weekends, I manage some doubles (or maybe that should be *Swipe Foursome*). But I enjoy watching Swipe, especially Wimbledon Swipe."'

'Good idea,' said Sharma. 'But with only a few games and many brands, how will it work?'

'The names will have to rotate,' said Barker, 'just as the tournament names do today. Two years from now, tennis may not be called Swipe but Toshiba. Or Boeing. Or Louis Vuitton.'

'People will be confused,' objected Tan.

'They'll get used to it,' she said dismissively. 'And we shouldn't only stick to games. We should open individual events in athletics too. Imagine the Jaguar Sprint for the 100-metre race and the Duracell Long Lasting Marathon (with other brands naming the runs in between). Imagine the Cathay Pacific Flight for the long jump, the Speedo Spurt for 50-metre butterfly swim and so on.'

'Wow!' said Sharma. 'You're right. Branding bliss could be just around the corner.'

We all drank to that.

For the record

My friend Vijay Yadav and I were discussing world records. Inevitably the topic turned to Usain (Lightning) Bolt and his extraordinary feat of smashing the 100m record thrice in 15 months: a quick man in a hurry.

'I wish I could do the same,' said Vijay, a wistful look on this face.

I gasped. Vijay is built on the lines of a medium-sized wardrobe and leads a life of pleasant languor, which includes eating well and playing golf. He may be able to run 100 metres, but not all continuously on the same day.

He clarified that he was not hung up on sprinting. 'I want a world record in *anything*. Just one world record—that's all I ask.'

Ah, he was seeking the glamour of fame, the glitter of stardom, the glow of limelight…

'Why don't you try for a Guinness World Record?' I said, 'There are many categories to choose from, some right up your street. For example, you're fond of hot dogs, right?'

Vijay nodded. He is fond of most things edible.

'Can you eat seven hot dogs…'

'Yes!' He said but I hadn't finished my sentence.

'… in three minutes? Then you'll overtake the Japanese eating legend Takeru Kobayashi, who, by the way, has also eaten 64 tacos in 15 minutes, 83 dumplings in 8 minutes, 100 pork buns in 12 minutes, 17.7 pounds...'

'My God' said Vijay, 'He can out-eat a bear.'

'Actually he cannot. He lost to a 1089-pound Kodiak bear in an eating competition. In the time the bear gobbled 50 hot dogs, Kobayashi could only manage 31. They say he was very upset with the loss and went on an eating spree to vent out his frustration.'

'I need a less formidable foe, nearer home,' said Vijay. 'Any eating record by an Indian?'

'Yes! Can you hold 58 seedless grapes in your mouth? You'd snatch the record from Shobhit Saxena Keshvdass.'

'I can't.'

'Swallow 201 worms (each 10 cm long) in 30 seconds and trounce C. Manoharan Snake Manu.'

'Forget it. How about drinking? Like beer?'

I could vouch for Vijay's beer-guzzling skill, acquired in college and honed over the years. But, rather ironically, Guinness World Records, named after its brewery sponsor, no longer recognizes alcohol consumption prowess.

'The closest to drinking is to *eat* a drinking glass in 86 seconds and destroy Patesh Talukdar's record.'

Vijay preferred not to eat glass. He was a difficult man to please. I offered him other Guinness World Records waiting to be broken—like eating 212 cold tinned peas in 3 minutes using a cocktail stick, husking a coconut with his teeth in 28.05 seconds and training his dog to unwind a non-electric car window in 11.33 seconds—but he refused them all and walked away, dejected.

But when he called me a few weeks later, he was excited.

'Check out today's newspaper!' he cried and gave me the page number.

'Sorry,' I said a few moments later, 'I only see an article about some beauty company...'

'That's the one! Do you see the picture?'

I could see a mass of masks: hundreds of people wearing white facial contraptions of the type—if you believe the hype—that cleanses the pores, moisturizes the skin, strips out acne, peels away wrinkles and removes excess fat from the waist.

'I'm in the first row,' cried Vijay, 'fourth from the left!'

'I'll take your word for it. And is your face more beautiful?'

'I wasn't there for beauty treatment but to break a world record.'

Apparently the beauty company had organized the extravaganza, collecting 859 people to form the largest group applying facial masks assembled at any one time on the planet.

'I'm a Guinness World Record holder now,' Vijay said proudly.

I didn't want to dampen his spirits by pointing out that the record would not carry his name, only the beauty company's.

'The next time you visit, I'll show you the T-shirt from the event, stating the record very clearly. In fact, since you're a close friend,' he added with an air of magnanimity, 'I'll even allow you to take a picture alongside me wearing the T-shirt.'

Obviously I was thrilled.

Taking marketing to the bank

'THE NAME OF BANKING IS getting sullied,' said Rick Hamilton, scowling at his drink. 'People have forgotten that without banks, life as we know it would not exist.'

Yes, but many say it would be better, I thought. Out loud I said: 'After the housing bubble burst, people *are* feeling anti-banks I suppose.'

'Yes,' said Hamilton, taking a big sip from his glass. 'I'm keen to know what a marketing man such as yourself—who has also worked in advertising—thinks. How can we convince the public about the value we offer?'

I was attending a party at the residence of one of my tennis buddies, a banker and the guest list was studded with banking magnates. Rick Hamilton, I learnt from the man himself, was the CEO of Anytime Bank, an independent and successful bank in the USA. He was in Singapore to attend a banking conference.

'So,' I said, 'you want people to think positively about the banking industry as a whole?'

Hamilton snorted. 'Of course not! I want them to think positively only about Anytime Bank. I don't get paid big bucks to run the banking industry as a whole, do I? In fact,' he added with an evil grin, 'if people feel good about

Anytime, I rather like it if they think negatively about other banks.'

'Do you have an advertising agency to help you in marketing?'

'No,' said Hamilton. 'We have a communications manager who takes out a few print advertisements in Forbes every year.'

'And what do those advertisements say?'

'They talk about the fact that Anytime Bank was founded in 1982 by the famous banker Louis Patterson who had made millions as the CEO of American Bank. The slogan is *Anytime Bank—the sturdy bank that has been around.*'

'Well, first of all,' I said, 'the people who read Forbes probably already know about Anytime Bank and its former CEO Patterson and perhaps even admire both. For the broad public, even if Patterson made millions of dollars...'

'But he did!' Hamilton said reverently. 'He made more money in American Bank during the oil crisis than the next four big bankers combined!'

'That's what the public detests about bankers—that they make millions of dollars.'

'Really?' Hamilton sounded surprised.

'Yes. Your slogan says you've been around for long and implies that you've done well for yourself in this period. It does not say what you do for people.'

'We're not in the doing-good-for-people business,' said Hamilton. 'We're in banking, for God's sake! Isn't the fact that we've grown faster than any other bank in America enough for the broad public? Shouldn't they be happy to know we've acquired more customers in the last four years than the next five banks put together? We're the best and they should know it!'

Hamilton's voice was rising in indignation. I downed my drink and took another from a passing waiter. I explained that the image of Anytime Bank needed to change from 'big corporation making piles of money for itself' to 'caring partner for the common man'.

'Ah, you mean, we need to *project* a nice guy image to the public?' he said. 'Talk a different story. We can do that.'

That was not quite what I meant but I proceeded. 'You need to stand for something more than being sturdy and long-lasting like an old oak tree, something of value to the consumer, like reliability and steadfastness.'

I took a sip. I was feeling light-headed and creative. 'For example,' I said, 'you could use your name to your advantage and make your slogan something like: *Anytime Bank—bank on us anytime.* You could run a series of ads in daily newspapers that show the brand as part of the common man's life as he goes about his daily activities. For example, one ad could show him at his three-year old daughter's bedside at night reading her a story as she drifts to sleep. The headline could say: *Read her to sleep at bedtime. Bank on us anytime.* The copy would talk about your financial services, housing loans and other goodies for the common man; for example: *With Anytime, you can grow your money during good times and you can protect your income during bad times; in other words, you can bank on us anytime.* At the bottom you clinch the deal by repeating the slogan with the brand logo, i.e. *Bank on us. Anytime.*'

I looked up sheepishly, realizing that I had got carried away. If I had tried to say this when I was at the agency, the creative folks would have shut me up after my first sentence. But Hamilton was staring at me with mouth open.

'Terrific stuff!' he said. 'Go on!'

I downed my drink and continued—the words seemed to flow effortlessly from my whisky-lubricated tongue. 'In the second ad the same man is on the golf course, sinking a twenty-foot punt. The headline says: *Sink that twenty-footer at putting time. Bank on us anytime.* No, golf is too elitist. Let's show him on the tennis court hitting a stunning serve that leaves his opponent stranded. The headline says: *Serve an ace at tennis time. Bank on us anytime.* The possibilities are endless. Watching sunset with arm around wife. *Enjoy a romantic moment at sunset time. Bank on us anytime.* Playing football with son. *Score a goal during bonding time. Bank on us anytime.*'

Hamilton was beaming. 'My God! This is good stuff. We can use your slogan. But more importantly, we can you use you! Will you join us in the USA as chief marketing officer?'

I explained that while I was flattered, I was a marketer, not a banker. But he said that what banking needed today was marketing. He spoke eloquently and the salary he offered spoke more eloquently than him. I was tempted: after all, banking was a lucrative industry, a Day One industry for recruitment at IIMA, in fact. And like every other MBA man worth the degree, I did not allow the fact that I was coasting along happily at Gronollers to preclude me being constantly on the look-out for something better.

While I was ruminating thus, he threw in the clincher argument.

'Look,' he said, 'Why not try it for six months? Don't move your family to New York yet. Do that only if you like it during this period. If it doesn't work out, simply walk out with a fat guaranteed bonus that we put into the contract. Sounds good?'

I nodded.

'During these six months,' he continued, 'I want you to understand what we do and prepare the right public relations and marketing plan based on this. You will join me and my two trusted colleagues Tim Richardson and Kevin Mayer in every major meeting so you can feel the pulse of the bank and how I run it.'

Medically speaking

THAT NIGHT, AFTER VERBALLY ACCEPTING Rick Hamilton's generous offer to join Anytime Bank on an initial six-month contract (he said the formal offer would follow), I found it difficult to go to sleep, thinking about my upcoming stint in a new city doing a new job without the family. Vidya, while not ecstatic about the news, had accepted it calmly enough ('At least I don't have to relocate to New York with the kids') and was now fast asleep. I needed something to calm the mind; my usual reading—a grisly whodunit—would not do it. So, browsing the internet for some soporific reading, I chanced upon some medical articles. I began reading and soon realized that medical progress is wonderful: what I was reading in the articles would no doubt save lives and alleviate pain. I did not realize that they would also bring me two fringe benefits soon.

At a party a few days later, thanks to some excellent fodder I'd gathered from the first article, I was able to add sparkle to a dull evening and, as a result, sparkle myself.

'Did you know that drinking whisky can protect you from cancer?' I said, timing my remark for the moment the host was filling everyone's glasses with Glenfiddich single malt. 'Dr Jim Swan, in a recent conference of EuroMedLab...'—the conference had taken place in 2005 but relative to the history of mankind, 2005 is pretty recent—'...announced that whisky contains a strong antioxidant that kills cancer cells. In fact, single malt has more ellagic acid—that well-known nemesis of cancer cells—than even red wine!'

My announcement was well-received. There's nothing that excites a group of drinkers more than evidence that suggests they drink more. The party cheered me with a hearty *'Bottoms up!'* and exhorted the host to perform his glass-filling miracle again.

'In Ladakh,' I continued, 'the Indian Army apportions rum to soldiers to cope with the severe cold. Whisky would be better, but the Army can't afford it... certainly not this fine single malt.'

They cheered that too. Sitting outdoors on a balmy Singapore evening, perspiring gently in the humidity, we all agreed that there's nothing like whisky for severe winter.

***

The second article provided me with an even nicer fringe benefit: it enabled me to get out of tricky situation with my wife.

We had just finished dinner at a nice restaurant. I was feeling replete as I leaned back in my chair and heaved a gentle sigh of contentment, carefully not allowing it to deteriorate into a burp. We had ordered well but I had eaten better, ignoring the frowns of disapproval and the do-you-really-think-you-need-mores my wife had thrown my way. I had been on a roll, not allowing a full stomach to impede me. In fact I discovered that I had not yet stopped rolling, so I got ready to order dessert. But getting this order past the wife was not easy. Unless, I thought, she isn't present when the order is taken.

'Aren't you going to the powder room?' I asked, 'There seems to be something on your chin.'

'No, there isn't,' she said, staring past me. 'You should get your eyes checked.'

I'd forgotten the wall behind me was a polished mirror. I realized the situation called for a more devious approach and suddenly I recollected my recently acquired medical knowledge. The waiter behind her was approaching us with the dessert menu. I encouraged him on with a smile; then turned to my wife, replacing the smile with a frown.

'Talking about eyesight,' I said, 'I'm very angry with Surender Singh. At a meeting today in office, he raised all sorts of awkward questions during my presentation, questions that hadn't occurred to the boss. It made me look stupid in the few days I'm still with Gronollers before handing in my resignation. I'm so angry, I may hit him tomorrow. What I need,' I quickly went on, knowing that if I gave her a chance, she would point out that I had never hit anyone previously, 'is something sweet.'

My timing was perfect. The waiter had just reached our table and, as my wife grappled with my seemingly preposterous statement, I quickly made my selection—*rasamalaai*, for the record—and sent the waiter scurrying away.

'You may be wondering,' I continued, 'about the connection between my hitting Surender and eating something sweet. Well, I read this medical report that says that a sugar rush provides the brain with the fuel it needs to push away thoughts of blame and revenge, making it easier for us to forgive and forget. The research was done at the University of Kentucky and these researchers—renowned scientists of impeccable stature—say that if the brain is short on sugar, it will not be able to keep vengeful impulses at bay.'

'What about the connection between your eyesight and Surender?' my wife asked, 'I was wondering about that too.'

'Oh, that? He wears spectacles, right? So when you said I need to get my eyes checked, I thought about specs, which then made me think about Surender and immediately my blood boiled. God, I needed this.'

I sunk my teeth into the *rasamalaai*, which the waiter had discreetly placed in front of me while we were talking.

'I can't believe this is true,' said my wife. 'And in any case, there's no reason to eat the sweet *now*. You only need to control your anger when you see him tomorrow.'

'You make a good point,' I said, gently dabbing my mouth with a napkin and looking with regret at my empty plate. 'I'll make sure I have some chocolate handy when I'm at work tomorrow.'

Banking on money

'I've called this meeting today,' announced Rick Hamilton, CEO of Anytime Bank as his two senior executives and I sat around the expensive walnut round table in his elegant Manhattan office, 'to discuss the disturbing news in this morning's paper.'

I had joined Anytime Bank and moved to New York on a six-month trial after my conversation with Hamilton in Singapore a couple of months ago. In those two months I had implemented the recommendations I had made over a drink to Hamilton in Singapore, unimpeded by an advertising agency to block my creativity. The bank's slogan was now: *Bank on us. Anytime.* The press advertisements I had described to Hamilton were running, more or less on the lines I had originally envisaged. And true to his word, Hamilton was getting me an orientation into the inner workings of the banking machinery by having me sit—mainly as an observer—in important meetings, like this one, which he had called suddenly at 10 am. The two colleagues with me were Tim Richardson, the senior managing director of risk management, and Kevin Mayer, executive director—finance, both close confidantes of Hamilton.

Tim Richardson looked puzzled.

'I checked the stock prices on CNN,' he said, 'as I do every morning before getting ready for work. I also read the Wall Street Journal over breakfast. I saw nothing to worry about. The Nikkei is stable. Commodity prices are holding.'

Kevin Mayer nodded. 'I too saw nothing untoward in the morning news.'

'Did you read the sports section?' asked Hamilton. They shook their heads. I could see what they were thinking: there is little money to be made by reading that section, so why waste time on it in the morning?

'It's about this baseball player Gil Meche,' Hamilton continued. 'He is a client of the bank. He had a contract, a perfectly legitimate legal document, which guaranteed him a $12 million salary in 2011. All he had to do was report for spring training next month, undergo surgery to repair his injured shoulder and turn up for games. He did not have to play.'

'Tell me about it,' said Mayer, 'Meche has it made. His team Kansas City Royals has some other players who…'

'May I continue?' Hamilton asked coldly.

'Yes, sorry.'

'As I said, all Meche had to do was turn up and collect the money. Do you know what he did? He did not.'

'Sorry Rick, I lost you there,' said Mayer.

'He didn't turn up, man! He retired last week, which means he will not be paid. No twelve million dollars. Zilch. And listen to what he says: "When I signed my contract, my main goal was to earn it. Once I started to realize I wasn't earning my money, I felt bad. I was making crazy amounts of money without even pitching."'

I glanced at Hamilton's two lieutenants. They looked

stunned. Then Richardson reached for the paper and placed it between himself and Mayer. Together they read it quickly, and then passed it to me as an afterthought. I scanned it quickly.

'Is it a joke?' asked Mayer.

'I thought it was some publicity stunt too,' said Hamilton, 'But no, it's verified. The idiot is actually not taking the money due to him.'

'My God! I can't believe it,' said Richardson. 'How can any idiot refuse money that is actually coming his way? I need a drink.'

'It's 10.15 in the morning, gentlemen,' said Hamilton, walking to the sideboard, 'But emergency situations call for emergency procedures.'

Soon we were sipping bourbon on the rocks.

'In my twenty three years in banking,' said Richardson, 'I've never heard anything so bizarre. Listen to what Meche says: "Honestly, I didn't feel like I deserved it." What do you think he means by "deserved"?'

'That really baffles me,' said Hamilton. 'I haven't heard that word for a long time so I looked it up. The dictionary says: justly or rightly earned; merited; as in a *deserved* increase in salary.'

'But that tells us nothing,' said Richardson, who had probably been at the receiving end of a salary increase every year for the last twenty, 'about why he is refusing his merited salary.'

'Exactly,' said Hamilton.

'What is the world coming to?' asked Mayer.

'Is he deranged?' asked Richardson.

'He is divorced,' said Hamilton. 'But so am I. No, he appears to be quite sane and that's the problem. What if other baseball players start refusing money they don't 'deserve'?

What if the disease spreads to other sportsmen? What if we suddenly have hoards of these fellows refusing money they have not 'earned'? The public may start demanding that more people who earn big bucks refuse money that they don't 'deserve'. Naturally everyone's attention will turn to us bankers.'

'What?!' cried Mayer, 'You mean...'

'Yes! They'll say, "Your bank made a huge loss last year and was nearly bankrupt. The government had to rescue you with bailout money. You should refuse your bonus salary."'

'No!' cried Richardson and Mayer together in anguish.

'Yes. Unless we do something, gentlemen, things will get out of hand, which brings me to the reason for this meeting. As I said, Gil Meche is our client. Gary Brooks is the relationship manger. Get Brooks to speak to him today and drill some sense into him.'

'What if he refuses to listen?'

'Tell Brooks to offer him a cash incentive.'

Culture shock in Tokyo

RICK HAMILTON HAD SENT ME to Tokyo to observe Anytime Bank's Japan operation. My plan was to fly back to New York after spending the weekend with my family in Singapore.

Soon after landing in Tokyo, I received the first shock of many. It was when I was in the line waiting for a taxi behind a balding European in a business suit.

I smiled at him and asked, 'How much is a taxi?'

'About US$250,' he said.

Thinking I had misled him by the wording of my question, I explained that I was not interested in buying the taxi. He clarified that he was talking about the taxi fare; then, as he saw my jaw sagging, he suggested I take the train if I wanted a cheaper option. I said I would, thanked him and moved away. Even on Anytime's expense account, my good-old Indian sensibilities would not allow me to squander over 10,000 rupees on a car ride.

At the train ticket counter, I learnt that this 'cheap' option would still set Anytime back by $45. I paid up and boarded the sleek Narita Express. As it slid out of the station—on the scheduled time to the dot—I leaned back in my comfortable chair car, stretched my legs and began to relax. Closing my eyes, I could almost imagine I was sitting alone in a monastery: it was that quiet and still. In reality, I was hardly still. The train was zipping fast through hills and forests dotted by small residential colonies and golf courses, but it seemed to be gliding soundlessly as if its wheels were made of foam. And I was far from alone: the train was almost full of passengers but they were reading quietly and talking so gently that I wondered if they actually spoke words or simply relied on lip reading.

In the midst of this church-like silence, my cell phone rang.

'*Saare jahaan se achaa, Hindustaan hamara, hamaara,*' screamed the singer in a rich voice. (I had proudly taken this ring-tone from a friend visiting New York from Mumbai.) My neighbour, an elderly Japanese man in a dark suit, jumped.

'Hello, hello!' I yelled into the receiver, 'Yes, I reached safely.'

It was my wife wanting to know how the New York-Tokyo flight was and when I'd be landing in Singapore. I babbled on about the flight, the weather, the horrendous taxi prices, the smooth train journey, the absence of any noise in the compartment... I stopped. I noticed the sign on the wall for the first time: 'Please leave the compartment if you wish to use your mobile phone.' Now the silence was deafening. Even the gentle lip movement had stopped. People stared stonily at the seat in front of them. My neighbour had stiffened like a wrinkled cardboard left too long in the sun. It seemed as if he had stopped breathing.

Mortified, I immediately tried to end the call, but in panic, pressed the 'loudspeaker' button instead. Into the silence, Vidya's voice, powerful at the best of times, boomed through the speaker: 'WHAT HAPPENED? WHY ARE YOU QUIET?'

Whispering 'Hold on' into the mouthpiece, I slunk out of the carriage.

At Shinjuku station, I jumped into a taxi and for a mere $10 was whisked to the hotel one kilometre away. There I was greeted with a deferential bow by the receptionist. I didn't want him to think we Indians are not taught manners, so I bowed right back. In response, he bowed again. I was a bit flummoxed about the correct response to this. Playing it safe, I bowed again. So did he. Finally, after we had bowed to each other several times, I decided to break the deadlock and asked him if he had a room for me. If he was disappointed that our game was ending so soon, he handled it stoically, completing my check-in formalities and handing me a key. I requested him to send an ironing board and an iron to the room.

My room was small—the double bed appeared to fill the floor area but on closer inspection, I found there was space to walk around it if I moved sideways. Soon Housekeeping delivered my ironing apparatus and I got another surprise. There was nothing wrong with the iron except that the knobs were labelled in Japanese but, instead of a foldable ironing table, I had been given a thin rectangle block, about the size of an A3 paper, covered in white cloth. I realized this was a Japanese space-saving strategy to cope with expensive real estate in Tokyo. It's a neat trick but unfortunately the board is designed for Japanese-sized shirts. My shirt overflowed on all sides. I had to iron it a few square inches at a time, painstakingly manoeuvring the iron over the shirt while the board kept sliding on the bed. When I examined my finished handiwork, I could not see much difference—absence-of-crease wise—between it and the next shirt waiting its turn for the iron. So I abandoned the project with some relief.

I then visited the toilet in my room and got my next shock. The toilet seat looked like a technological marvel designed by NASA. There was a control panel on the seat with many buttons labelled in Japanese. As I raised the seat, the whole structure responded by making a gurgling but not unfriendly noise. I continued to gaze at it in wonder as I brushed my teeth and changed into my night clothes.

Later as I gently lowered myself on to my bed, I was almost relieved that a Japanese lullaby did not automatically start playing from hidden speakers in the wall.

Taking taxi trips in Tokyo

'THIS IS THE HOTEL YOU'LL be staying in,' Barbara Holt, my administration assistant at Anytime Bank, had said before I left New York. She had given me my itinerary. 'And this is the address of Anytime Bank in Tokyo. But knowing the address in Japan is not enough: you need to have it in writing, in Japanese. So I've prepared this for you.' The good woman had handed me another folder: I could see the writing was Japanese.

On the first day, there were no taxis in the hotel driveway. The doorman explained that there were plenty plying on the main road 100 metres away and he could call for one for me. Waving the sheet with my destination printed in Japanese, I told him I was thoroughly capable of walking 100 metres and finding a taxi on my own. I walked jauntily to the main road, hailed a passing cab, got in and handed over the printed card to the driver with aplomb.

I expected the cabbie to immediately whisk me away to the address as Holt had said he would but he turned around and, pointing to the paper in his hand, said something to me, very politely… in Japanese. I listened patiently and, when he finished, nodded equally politely and said, 'Yes.'

He spoke some more, pointed to something on the paper and asked me something.

'Yes,' I said, nodding some more.

He gesticulated at the paper vigorously. Not to be outdone, I nodded more vigorously.

Finally, he shook his head in disgust, said what sounded suspiciously like 'Idiot!' in Japanese, took off and drove me straight back to my hotel. Pressing a button, he opened my door. I took out my wallet but he waved me away, his hands clearly saying, 'I don't need your stupid money. Just get out of my cab!' As soon as I did, he drove away.

'Why did he not take me here?' I asked the doorman, handing him the card.

'He did, sir. This is the hotel address.'

Oh my God! I remembered: Holt had also printed the hotel address in Japanese so I could return easily in the evening.

'This time,' said the doorman, 'let me hail a cab for you, sir.'

'Yes!' I said, 'Why don't you do that? And let me bring the correct address from my room.'

I raced up two flights of stairs to my room and returned just as a cab drove in.

This time when I handed the address to the cabbie, he smiled, entered it into the car's GPS system and drove off.

Meanwhile, I was perspiring from my recent exertion.

'It's hot!' I said.

The cabbie looked at me in his rear-view mirror and smiled.

'Very hot!' I said. He smiled some more.

I waved my hands as if I were fanning my face. He waved back to me in the mirror, grinning broadly. Obviously, driving an Indian—that too, such a happy one—was a novel experience for him and he was enjoying it.

I leaned forward and pointed at his dashboard.

'AC! AC!' I said, speaking slowly.

He laughed and shook his head. 'No AC. GPS,' he explained, pointing to the screen.

'No, AC! AC!' I said and pointed to the duct below the GPS screen. 'Very hot!'

'Hot-oh?!' he said. Aha! I was getting through at last. Over a slow conversation with the Japanese bartender at the hotel bar the previous night, I had learnt that the Japanese frequently add the 'oh' sound to English words.

'Yes! Hot-oh!' I said.

He turned the knob two inches to the right. I leaned back in relief and waited for the icy breeze. It didn't come. In fact, I was feeling stuffier and had begun to perspire freely.

Then it hit me. Thinking I wanted it hotter, he had turned on the heater!

'No!' I said. 'Hot-oh! Hot-oh!' He smiled.

I took off my coat to demonstrate I was feeling hot. But somehow this made him think I now needed even more heat. He turned the knob fully to the right. I felt like pizza in an oven. My shirt was sticking to my body. I could see beads of perspiration on the cabbie's neck too but he was bearing it stoically.

Finally, I removed my seat belt, leaned over the front seat and turned the air-conditioner knob all the way to the left.

'Now OK-oh!' I said. 'Don't stop-oh. Drive to destination-oh.'

The quest for a new toilet seat

ON MY FIRST NIGHT IN Tokyo, I had been intimidated by the toilet seat and had approached it warily the next morning. But as I lowered myself gingerly on to the seat, I got a pleasant surprise: the seat was warm and welcoming. As soon as I had sat down, a deep gurgling sound had started. The buttons were all labelled in Japanese but when my work was done, I fiddled with them and till I figured out how to experience the soothing pleasure of a warm shower wash, I was addicted.

For the next two days in Japan, I enjoyed my new addiction (as toilets in office buildings, restaurants and public areas were equipped with the same technological wonder). I resolved to buy a similar seat for our toilet in Singapore.

Over the weekend in Singapore, therefore, I excitedly told my wife we needed to go shopping and she reacted positively. Her enthusiasm waned when she learnt that my quest was for a new toilet seat, but she was trapped in the car by then.

At a high-end sanitary ware retail shop, I told the saleswoman, 'I'm looking for a toilet seat that, um... offers washing facilities.'

'You mean a shower wash?' she asked.

'Yes!'

She showed me an ordinary toilet seat with a separate shower hose dangling on the side.

'You mean, physically hold the hose in the hand and navigate it?' I asked, 'That's so rudimentary.'

My wife tried to tell me that a hand-shower costing $40 was adequate for our needs but I would have none of it.

'I'm looking for the advanced version, you know, like in Japan.' I told the saleswoman.

'Oh you mean the Washlet S400, sir? Follow me.'

She took me to a seat that looked like the one in Japan... then I noticed the panel on the side with buttons and lights was missing.

'Oh no! Where are the controls?!' I cried in panic.

'Here.' She put a small square box—about six inches on each side and two inches thick—into my hands. It was a remote control with all the requisite knobs.

'They've stopped making the old version with the panel attached to the seat, sir,' she explained.

I cradled the remote control in my hands and started getting used to its feel.

'Nice,' I said, 'How much?'

'$2,795, sir.'

My jaw dropped. I scratched my head, trying to think this one through. If we bought one today and used it, say, twice a day for the next twenty years, the cost per use would be approximately...

I was interrupted from my deep analysis by a sharp tap on my shoulder.

'Don't even think of buying this contraption,' said my wife. 'Let's buy the simple hand shower, which is fixed to the wall and cannot get lost. Do we really need one more remote control in the house?'

My God! The woman is right. We have remote control units for too many things in the house already. I'm constantly misplacing the remote control for the air conditioners (I recently found one in my laptop bag, tucked away near the charger). As for the four remote controls that we have to operate one television set, not only do I keep misplacing these, I'm also using them incorrectly, pressing the DVD play button to increase the television volume or the channel changer to find my car keys.

In my mind's eye, I see myself seated on the new toilet seat, mission accomplished, reaching luxuriously for the remote control and encountering empty space. Or I imagine I'm watching television: I reach for the remote and of course pick up the wrong one. But this time, instead of the DVD player ejecting a disc, water is squirted on an unsuspecting guest in the bathroom. Then I think: what if water squirts on me from the television set? You never know with gadgets these days.

'You're right,' I told Vidya. 'Let's stick to the simple hand shower.'

We don't tolerate conflict of interest here

BACK IN NEW YORK THE following week, I entered the office of Rick Hamilton, CEO of Anytime Bank. As soon as I saw him, I knew he was in a bad mood.

'You wanted to see me?' I said as I sat down. He looked up and grimaced in pain. 'What happened?' I asked. 'Are you sick?'

'Much worse!' he snapped. 'Yesterday, I sold 200,000 shares of Cobalt Cornwalis at $63.47 each, shares I had picked up at $5.79 two months ago—when Anytime had sanctioned Cornwalis' loan to expand their business.'

That sounded like insider trading but I thought it best not to mention it. 'Wow!' I said. 'The sale must have netted you—let me see—close to $11.5 million in profit. Well done!'

'No!' He scowled. 'I sold them on Rupert Baxter's advice. Idiot! I should have waited another day. The Cornwalis' share price is $64.22 today. I could have earned $150,000 more. I always like to make $150,000 more.'

His secretary walked into his office.

'Anyway, where's everybody?' he barked at her as he always did when he was in a bad mood. (Come to think of it, I had also seen him do it when he was in a good mood, perhaps to stay in practice). 'The meeting was to start five minutes ago.'

'They're waiting in the meeting room as you wanted,' the good woman said.

'Okay, let's go,' he said to me. 'Why are you still sitting here?'

We entered the meeting room adjacent to his office. If Hamilton was contrite at keeping his two lieutenants—Tim Richardson, the senior managing director of risk management, and Kevin Mayer, executive director finance—waiting, he hid it well. Nodding gruffly, he sat down and began the meeting.

'First: when is Broody's submitting their credit ratings of the two instruments we packaged up last week?'

'Friday,' said Richardson.

'Will they be AAA?'

'Of course.' Richardson sounded offended at being asked such a basic question. 'Broody's will get their usual exorbitant fee. In addition, their finance controller's son, who is graduating from school this year and joining Purdue, will receive Anytime Bank's Education Scholarship for Academic Achievers.'

'Excellent!' said Thornton. 'Next topic: I need to get back to the Board on the compensation question: should the bank's bonus structure be changed to reward long-term results?'

'How long-term?' asked Kevin Mayer.

'Around 10 years.'

'What?! I'd get my next bonus in 2021?'

'No, you chum, you'd get it this year. However it would be based on the performance of the investments you made 10 years ago for the bank.'

'Let me see,' said Mayer. 'Wasn't it 10 years ago that we designed and sold truckloads of those sub-prime fellows?'

'Yes.'

'And they're all bust now.'

'Exactly,' said Hamilton, 'And on that basis, you *will not* receive a bonus this year. Neither will I.'

'It's a stupid idea!' cried Mayer, 'Who suggested it?'

'The government, I believe.'

They spent a few minutes voicing their opinions—uniformly negative—on the government.

'How is the government in India, Jags?' Hamilton asked, turning to me. 'As stupid as this?'

'Well,' I said, 'on occasion, they have been known to...'

'Exactly!' said Hamilton. 'Now let's return to the issue at hand. I need a convincing argument to tell the Board to leave bonuses as they are. Kevin, please do the analysis showing why this proposal won't work. Throw in a few bar charts showing what other banks are doing: the Board loves bar charts.'

'Sure,' said Mayer. 'I'll also get HR to give me some spiel about how motivation works better in the short-term versus the long-term.'

'Great idea! Get bar charts on that too. Next: talking of HR, they're proposing we move the office to the new Sandown Commercial Estate area. Apparently it has everything we need, is near a subway station and far enough from Manhattan to cost only a fifth in rent.'

'But I live six blocks from here!' cried Kevin Mayer in anguish.

'I know,' said Hamilton, and surprised me by giving Mayer a big wink. 'Don't I remember the party you threw there in January? It was before you joined us, Jags. The girls were gorgeous...'

'Thanks,' murmured Mayer.

'I too stay only two blocks from here,' said Hamilton. 'So what do we say to HR?'

'Leave it to me,' said Mayer grimly. 'I'll put together statistics showing that businesses in this location have a higher revenue-generating ability because of the strategic proximity to capital markets...'

'Wow! Do we have such data?' asked Hamilton.

'No. But I'll put Quantum Questions on the job. They depend on our bank for a lot of research—they will happily churn out whatever's necessary.'

'Superb! I'll tell HR that it's a wonderful idea but before we embark on it, I've commissioned a robust cost-benefit analysis, which we can review in a couple of weeks. Okay, gentlemen, last topic on the agenda, also from HR. It's about your secretary Louise Peterson, Bill. Apparently she has given an order for stationery worth $20,000 to Bionic Stationers. It turns out the company belongs to her husband.'

'Oooh!' said Richardson.

'Exactly,' said Hamilton. 'We've detailed our policy clearly in our employee handbook. Sorry, Bill, we have to let her go. We don't tolerate conflict of interest at Anytime Bank.'

The flying go-getter gets going

'YOUR FLIGHT TO NEWARK IS delayed by ninety minutes, sir,' the clerk at Chicago's O'Hare airport told me. As a flying go-getter I immediately looked around me for other options.

A go-getter is an aggressively enterprising person full of energy and tenacity, who achieves stuff. He surmounts obstacles strewn across his path and moves on, exhibiting carpe diem at the drop of a hat. A go-getter just goes... at a frantic pace.

Normally I'm not a go-getter. When faced with an important decision—like whether to order *gobi manchurian* wet or dry—I dither and dawdle. If a leaking kitchen sink needs fixing, for example, I first ascertain if it *really* needs to be done ('Can't we place a cup underneath to capture the leaking water?'), and only when convinced (by my wife's icy look), will I do something about it, slowly, in the next few weeks.

But when I fly, I become a full-fledged go-getter, intent on moving fast and winning the race to the destination. Since I'm not allowed to fly the aircraft, I look for other ways to fly faster, like trying to catch an earlier flight and, when the plane lands, racing my fellow passengers to the terminal.

Three months had passed with Anytime Bank and I was taking a few days' leave, flying first to Singapore and then going with my family for a holiday. But just before my leave started, Hamilton had asked me to fly to Chicago with him for a meeting. So I was taking the flight back to New York (Hamilton would remain in Chicago for another day), from where I was catching a connection to Singapore.

I was unhappy that my 5 pm flight would depart only by 6.30, meaning I would land in Newark airport at 9.30 pm. Apart from my natural go-getter inclination to fly faster, I was also afraid of missing the connection at Newark. As the famous saying goes, 'a delayed flight often gets delayed more'. Other passengers on my connection also looked worried, but while they merely stood in a group and discussed their predicament, I *acted*.

Swiftly scanning the flight information, I found another United Airlines flight leaving at 5.30 pm for New York's La Guardia airport. I grabbed my luggage and ran to the gate at the other end of the airport, arriving there panting after a ten-minute jog. I joined the last five standby passengers in queue. By the time I got my breath back, only two were ahead of me. I asked the lady in front of me how long it would take to travel from La Guardia airport to Newark airport by taxi.

'Why don't you simply fly directly to Newark airport?' she asked.

'Long story. Flight delayed. Need to make connection.' I was curt because one, she didn't really need this information and two, the person ahead of her was almost done, 'Just tell me how long it will take.'

'Perhaps an hour,' she said vaguely.

I started calculating in my head: land at 8.30 pm, one hour taxi ride...

'Sir, we're about to close the doors,' the agent said, 'I have a seat. Do you want it?'

'Yes!' I said. (Go-getters make momentous decisions in a split second much to the awe of the people around them.)

I trotted into the aircraft and found my seat. Immediately the doors closed, the aircraft started moving and I started congratulating myself on my quick running and firm decisiveness. I was still congratulating myself when the aircraft came to a stop after 10 minutes. 15 minutes later, I stopped congratulating myself: it was 6 pm.

At 6.10, the flight attendant announced that there was 'an unforeseen delay and we'll be stuck here for a while—sorry!'

In shock, I approached her. 'I have a connection at 11 pm at Newark!' I said.

'But this flight goes to La Guardia!' she said, 'Why didn't you take the direct flight to Newark?'

'That flight was delayed.'

'Well, now this one is,' she said and laughed. I could see nothing funny in the situation. In a cold voice I asked her to check with the captain when our flight would take off.

'Why don't you talk to him directly, sir? I'm sure he'll enjoy the joke too.'

Still giggling, she escorted me to the pilot's cabin. I explained my predicament to the captain.

'We're all ready to fly,' he said, 'But there's some union-enforced slowdown in La Guardia, so *all* flights are delayed. We're now scheduled to depart at 7 pm.'

'Oh no!' I said, 'What about my original 5 pm flight to Newark? That was delayed by 90 minutes, but with this union trouble, it will be stuck for a long, long time, right?'

'The union situation is only at La Guardia; Newark is fine. Here's your flight.' He pointed to his computer screen.

'It has been cleared for take-off and should be taxiing out any minute now.'

We finally landed at La Guardia at 9.30 pm. I sprinted to the taxi stand by 9.45 and, by promising him $50 extra if he made the journey in one hour, got the cabbie to drive like the devil. We made it in 55 minutes but the aircraft doors had closed with my fellow passengers—who had exhibited no initiative, no gumption, no velocity, no go-getter trait—safely inside.

As I took the next day's flight to Singapore I thought: I'm used to not being rewarded for my glorious efforts, but to be *punished* like this was gross injustice.

The two secrets of marriage compatibility

My go-getter behaviour having misfired, I arrived later than planned in Singapore and had to scramble to get the family ready for our holiday in Europe. We had never been on an exotic holiday before but I decided we had to go because *everyone* we knew seemed to have done it. In parties, we were constantly meeting people who had 'enjoyed the skiing in the Swiss Alps'; had been 'bowled over by the wine in France'; had 'spent a full day at the London museum'; or had 'zipped down the German autobahn at 150 kilometres per hour'.

So here we were on the first leg of the vacation in Milan in Italy. Vidya and I had just checked into a hotel while our children stayed with my daughter's Italian classmate, whose home was in this city (and apparently filled with her cousins visiting on a holiday). Alone with my wife, I got to practice the two secrets of marriage compatibility I had learnt through a painful process of trial and error over the years: knowing when to (1) agree to disagree and (2) disagree to agree with her.

'Nice and cool,' I murmured on entering our hotel room.

'Freezing!' my wife cried.

I was surprised. 'Okay, why don't you get into bed and under the quilt? And wrap an extra blanket around your head?'

'I will not lie covered in bed like an Eskimo. Adjust the AC.'

I was not sure Eskimos lie covered in bed. In fact I was not even sure they had beds. But I merely said, 'Okay' and turned the thermostat from 20^{0}C to 21^{0}C.

'It's still freezing,' she complained a few minutes later and insisted on checking the thermostat herself, 'No wonder! It's set at 21^{0}.'

She turned the machine off completely. The room began to warm up; so, when she wasn't looking, I switched it on again. But later, when I came out of the bathroom, the room felt summery and stifling. She had turned off the air conditioner *and* opened all the windows.

'Okay,' I said, sitting across her on the bed and adopting the reasonable attitude of husband-who-understands. 'Let's agree to disagree on what is the right temperature of this room. I like it cool and comfortable but you seem to like it stuffy and sweltering. I suggest...'

'No!' she interrupted me. '*I* like it cool and comfortable. You seem to like it frigid and freezing.'

'Okay, okay,' I said soothingly. 'Let's not quibble. Why not say I like it slightly chilly and you like it slightly stuffy?' Before she could contest even this reasonable statement, I continued quickly: 'Why don't we compromise? And set the temperature at 22^{0}C?'

'26^{0},' she said.

'23.'

'25.5'

'I'm going up one degree each time: you're only reducing by half!'

'I'm not haggling!' she said, '25.5°C or I'm going out.'

'Okay—you know where the door is.' Being chivalrous by nature, I did not say this. Instead I convinced her to agree to 25° and, after she had gone to sleep, I placed an extra blanket over her and set it back to 22°.

She noticed it the next morning and switched off the machine again. But as we left the room, I surreptitiously switched it on, so it was deliciously cool when we returned that evening.

'It's freezing!' she screamed and promptly turned it off and opened the windows. We went through yesterday's rigmarole again. But it was all done in a cordial, agree-to-disagree spirit.

The next morning I got the opportunity to practise the second secret of marriage compatibility with my wife: knowing when to disagree to agree with her.

She came out of her bath all dressed and ready to go but her face lacked the holiday sparkle. In fact she looked distinctly depressed.

'I've put on weight!' she cried. 'It shows in this new skirt and blouse I bought specially for this trip. Don't I look heavy here?' She pointed at her hips.

I told you I had learnt the two methods through trial and error... Well, early in our marriage, when faced with the same question, I had carefully looked at her hips, exactly as I had been asked, and after a judicious assessment, had agreed with her. Then I had proceeded to give her a couple of excellent weight-shedding tips. That day I learnt that such a response was foolhardy.

So today in Milan, I shook my head firmly and said: 'Sorry, I disagree to agree with you. You've not put on weight.'

'Are you sure?' she asked anxiously. 'You're not even looking at my hips. You're just saying this to please me.'

'No,' I said, disagreeing to agree with her once again. 'I'm not saying it to please you. You're looking fine. Slim, in fact. And beautiful,' I added. 'Now let's go—we have to pick up the kids in twenty minutes.'

A doctor for daughter

I TOLD MY DAUGHTER TWICE NOT to fall ill during our upcoming vacation. But when has a teenager ever listened to her father? So, choosing a particularly inconvenient place and time—Venice at midnight—she fell sick. As she lay in bed looking withered and forlorn, we decided to get her treated in Rome, our next destination. As we checked out of the hotel at the crack of dawn, I looked at our luggage and realized that walking to the pier to get a boat to the Venice railway station was going to be tricky.

'I'll carry your luggage and mine,' I said magnanimously to my daughter. She did not go berserk with gratitude.

'Oh, so no one is carrying *me*?' she said.

Arms and shoulders sore, I grappled with the bags on the half-kilometre walk on a path of cobbled stones that crossed the canals a few times before reaching the pier. We managed to reach the railway station and board the train to Rome. Soon after settling into our hotel, I called Reception about seeing a doctor.

'Of course, sir,' the man replied in gentle courtesy, 'The doctor can visit you within an hour. Shall I call him now?'

'How much will he charge?' I asked.

He replied in a calm, reassuring voice.

'Sorry,' I said, 'there's something wrong with the line. It sounded like you said €190.'

'I did, sir,' he said soothingly, 'Shall I call him now?'

'Alternatively,' I said, 'can we take her to a nearby hospital?'

'The nearest hospital is a government one, sir. It's free.'

'That's perfect! How do I get there?'

'No, sir, I meant it's free for *locals*. You can't go there with your foreign passports.'

I told him we would leave our passports in the hotel but it wasn't that easy: local identity cards had to be shown. There was no private clinic nearby and in any case, they weren't inexpensive. So I acquiesced to getting the doctor to visit us and conveyed the shocking figure of his fees to my wife.

Twenty minutes later, there was a knock on the door. But instead of the doctor, a tall, handsome man in his thirties stood there, with luxurious blonde hair, fashionable sunglasses and a carefully maintained two-day stubble. He was dressed in corduroy jeans and a navy blue Ralph Lauren t-shirt that fit him snugly, accentuating firm muscles.

I recoiled slightly under the impact of his powerful cologne and dazzling smile.

'This is room 621,' I said, 'Which room are you looking for?'

'I was told there is a sick girl there,' he said, a frown creasing his handsome brow.

Realization dawned. 'You're the doctor! You look like a Hollywood actor.'

He was pleased. The frown was replaced by the dazzling smile again.

'Which actor do I resemble?' he asked.

I explained that I hadn't quite meant a *particular* Hollywood specimen and asked him gently if he would like to examine the child now.

'Yes, yes, of course,' he said hastily and moved to my daughter's bedside. He quickly ran the stethoscope on her back and chest and used a torch to look at her tongue, finishing his examination in 90 seconds flat. I know because I timed him.

'It's nothing,' he said as he packed his instruments, 'Just mild sunstroke. Here, give her this medicine...'

He scribbled out a prescription as he talked for another 90 seconds, which included giving me directions to the pharmacy. Then he started filling out his invoice with considerable more interest that he had shown while examining the girl. I used the time to calculate that, at the rate of €190 per three minutes, the man made close to €4,000 for every hour he worked.

My wife obviously felt we should get more medical attention for our buck because she now spoke up: 'Actually, Doctor, she banged her head on the table two days ago—could you see if that could have anything to do with her condition today?'

Two days ago, my daughter had bent down to pick up an article she had dropped. This is something she did rarely—I mean the picking up, not the dropping—and when straightening, she had banged her head on the table. I knew the knock was nothing because she had bounced back quickly and asked me (again) to buy her a BlackBerry phone.

'Okay,' the Greek god said, shaking his blonde locks, 'Let me take a look.'

He quickly examined my daughter's skull and, raising her eyelids one at a time, peered into her eyes.

After 45 seconds of excruciating labour, he announced: 'No concussion. There is no injury to the head.'

He then took the invoice and, without flinching, added a line at the bottom. The total was now €240: €190 for the house call and €50 for 'special examination at the patient's request.'

'No wonder he can afford to dress so nattily,' I said to my daughter after he left.

'I know!' she said, perking up briefly. 'After you get me the BlackBerry, can you buy me D&G sunglasses like his?'

Lost in transportation

THE SECOND LEG OF OUR Europe holiday was Spain. I had just pulled out of the Barcelona airport rental car premises when my wife cleared her throat. I rolled my eyes, knowing exactly what she was going to say.

The question she was about to put to me is asked often by sociologists and scientists; by psychologists and philosophers; and by librarians and language teachers. But while these people may differ in profession and education, and perhaps even bone structure, they have one thing in common: they are all *women*, just like my wife. Here she goes, I thought.

'Why don't you ask for directions?' she said.

It occurred to me that the bigger, deeper question that needed probing was: *Why do women ask men to ask for directions*? But, giving Vidya no glimpse of the philosophical questions and other emotions stirring inside me, I answered patiently.

'Because we're not lost. Because we're entering the only highway to Barcelona. Because the sign says 'Barcelona' straight ahead.'

She did not cringe with shame and apologize. Instead she said, 'I know all that, but remember what happened in Milan two days ago? You drove out of the airport and...'

'Yes, yes, I remember,' I said quickly before she went into unnecessary detail in front of the children. 'But this is completely different. I know the way.'

And it turned out I did... approximately. I missed the exit and had to backtrack a few kilometres but in the process, was able to show everyone a truly magnificent park that we would never have glimpsed otherwise.

The next day was sunny and bright. A cool breeze welcomed us when we stepped out of the hotel. As we drove out of the hotel car park, I was feeling chirpy... until my wife dampened my mood with her query: 'Aren't you asking for directions?'

'No,' I replied, 'We're in the hotel driveway and there is only one way out.'

The map I had consulted before starting had been perfectly clear. I exited the hotel and entered the highway like a veteran of Barcelona. Sure enough, I soon saw signs pointing to my exit and pressed the accelerator with quiet command.

An hour later, I was less sure. For twenty minutes I had seen no sign of our exit. Continuing to smile breezily and giving no outward indication of panic, I said: 'I'm stopping for petrol... use the bathroom if you need to.'

Soon we all got back into the car.

'I was chatting with the petrol pump attendant while paying the bill,' I casually announced, 'And he said there's an alternative route just down the road.' I pointed vaguely in the direction we had come. Soon we were zipping down the highway again.

After I had ignored the first exit and the second and the third, my wife asked, 'Which exit?'

'Oh, we have ways to go,' I said, 'Another 22 kilometres.'

'So you lost your way 30 kilometres ago?'

My wife has this annoying trait of stating the obvious when there is really no need.

'Well, not exactly,' I said. 'I was on the right route. I just missed the exit.'

'I see. Perhaps you could have asked for directions 30 kilometres ago?'

What did I tell you? The same question... Unbelievable.

We returned to Singapore for the last weekend of my holiday before I was to head back to New York. Now, on a holiday, you may argue (especially if you're a woman) that asking the way in unfamiliar territory could provide additional insurance. But my wife did not stop when we were back home.

On Friday night, we were visiting a friend for the first time.

'Have you asked him how to get to his place?' she asked as soon as we left home.

'I've checked the map,' I said.

'But isn't it much easier to simply call him and ask for directions?'

There—once again! No logic, no reasoning, no thought... just a parrot-like repetition of the same question.

For some odd reason, the map did not direct me to his apartment straightaway—perhaps it was an older version—and I had to meander through a few streets before we arrived at his house. But it was no big deal. We were no more than 45 minutes late and one couple arrived even after we did. However, my wife still felt I should have asked for directions.

The next day, we left the house for a different party. Predictably, she said, 'Did you ask Piyush for directions?'

'We've been to Piyush's house before,' I said.

'Yes, I know. And you lost your way the last time.'

'Not exactly,' I said, 'Yes, I missed the right highway exit but we drove no more than 12 kilometres extra.'

'Singapore is 40 kilometres end to end,' she said, 'If you had driven a little more, we would have been lost in Malaysia. So to avoid a similar situation, why not call Piyush now and ask for directions?'

Perhaps I should invest in a GPS system for the car, I thought. As anyone could see, I didn't really need it, but I thought it might make the wife happy. And perhaps keep the dreaded question off her lips.

Avoiding the Goldman Sachs blunder

FOUR MONTHS INTO MY STINT at Anytime Bank, I was having coffee with the CEO Rick Hamilton. During the course of the conversation, he idly picked up the *New York Times* and glanced through it. As he did this, his mood darkened. He shouted for his secretary.

'Get Mayer and Richardson,' he snapped at her as she scurried in. 'And Howard Sklaryk too.' She scurried out. 'You stay,' he barked at me.

Soon Tim Richardson, the senior managing director of risk management, and Kevin Mayer, executive director finance, joined us in Hamilton's office. We were seated in the soft, luxurious sofa set that adorned one corner of the office, with an elegant coffee table in the centre. Hamilton had placed the *New York Times* on this.

While waiting for Howard Sklaryk, Anytime's Human Resources Manager, I read through the article Hamilton had marked on the Times' Op Ed page, 'Why I Am Leaving Goldman Sachs'. The writer Greg Smith, disgusted with what Goldman Sachs stood for, was quitting. In the opening paragraph, he described the working environment as *'toxic and destructive'*; a few lines later, he talked about how *'the interests of the client continue to be sidelined in the way the firm operates and thinks about making money.'*

It was hot stuff and I had just finished reading it when Sklaryk entered the office.

'Rick,' he said to Hamilton, 'I'm interviewing candidates. Can it wait?'

'No,' said Hamilton. 'Sit down.'

Sklaryk joined us on the sofa.

'Have you guys read the article by Greg Smith, who quit Goldman Sachs yesterday?' asked Hamilton, pointing to the paper.

'Yes!' said Mayer, laughing and picking up the Times, 'What a hilarious nut! Listen to this: "It makes me ill how callously people talk about ripping their clients off". The man must have been sick all the time! And then he says: "Call me old-fashioned, but I don't like selling my clients a product that is wrong for them". Old-fashioned, Greg?! You're a dinosaur!'

'Exactly,' said Hamilton, 'but I didn't call this meeting to have a laugh with you, Kevin.' Mayer stopped grinning. 'I want to know if we have walking time-bombs like Smith in Anytime.'

'No!' cried Richardson, Mayer, and Sklaryk in unison.

'But do we ensure it in our recruiting? Howard, you're interviewing our next batch of management trainees. How are you making sure none is a future Smith?'

'Our recruitment system is built on ensuring it, Rick. We go to the top universities, so we don't waste time evaluating these kids' financial acumen. We focus on gauging one important characteristic: a deep, burning desire for money that dominates all other motivations.'

'That's right on the money!' said Hamilton, 'By the way, the pun was intended. But how do you get the answer?'

'During the interview, we try to find out what the candidate will do to acquire wealth. For example, I just asked Jeremy Habit, the candidate I left behind in my room to answer your summons—' he gave Hamilton a look of reproach—it was wasted '—what he will do if he gets a phone call saying his grandmother is critically ill and he has to rush to the hospital or never see her alive; but as soon as he hangs up, he gets another call saying he has won $6,000 in a contest but has to collect the money in the next hour or lose it forever.'

'He collects the cash, of course,' said Tim Richardson, 'It's a no-brainer.'

'Yes! But amazingly, many candidates select the grandma. College toppers, but no sense of money. We weed them out straightaway. But I think we have an exceptional candidate in Habit. He said he'd ask if they would increase the pay-out to $10,000 if he made it in the next 15 minutes.'

'Mm,' said Hamilton, nodding his approval. I could see that Richardson and Mayer were impressed too.

'Exactly! He sounded too good to be true,' continued Sklaryk. 'So I tested him further by telling him this true recent story about a group of construction worker friends in New Jersey who regularly pooled their money to buy lottery tickets, which they entrusted to one member of the group, Americo Lopes. One day, Lopes quietly collected $17.5 million of after-tax prize money and did not tell his friends. I asked for his reaction. "I think Lopes did the right thing," he said, "given there was no written contract. His friends would have done the same in his place. After all, it's real money we're talking about." I now have a good assessment of Habit's money motivation and I'm bloody impressed.'

'So am I, so am I,' said Hamilton genially.

Sklaryk continued: 'I also ask candidates to name their hero. If the idiots say Mahatma Gandhi or Albert Einstein, they're out. We're looking for wealthy names here.'

'Between visiting a dying grandmother and collecting $6,000 from somewhere else, amazingly, many candidates select the grandma. College toppers, but no sense of money. We weed them out straightaway.'

'Of course!' said Hamilton, 'And who's Habit's hero?'

'Mitt Romney.'

'Sklaryk, our recruiting is in good hands. Next week let's go through our on-boarding, training and performance appraisal system and ensure that they too are geared to develop the right talent at Anytime Bank. Now go and finish interviewing Habit. It looks like you have a gem in your hands. I look forward to welcoming him into Anytime.'

fanatic football fever

IT WAS NOT UNTIL THE trip I took to London during my Anytime Bank stint that I really appreciated the football fan's passion for his game. For some reason the banking conference I was attending had been arranged at the hotel located at the Chelsea Football Club's stadium, Stamford Bridge. For my group of global managers—including Americans for whom football is a game where players use their hands and body to smash into other players (not always from the opposing team)—it was just another hotel. But for Chelsea fans it was a hallowed venue worthy of worship.

I realized this when, soon after checking in on a Friday afternoon, I asked for the way to the gym.

'Walk past the stadium, sir.' The receptionist gave me time to grasp the enormity of this stroll. 'And you'll reach the Chelsea Club gym.'

'Thanks,' I said, 'It's free for hotel guests, of course?'

'No, sir!' The man was shocked. 'This is the *Chelsea Club* gym, part of the *Stamford Bridge Stadium*. Entry is £25 pounds.'

I gasped.

'But for hotel guests,' he continued in the tone of a monarch bequeathing a purse of gold to a lowly subject, 'it's only £20.'

I avoided the gym, but later thought I would imbibe some of this football spirit, even if it meant spending some money. I went to the ticket counter at the stadium.

'There's a match here this Sunday, right?' I said brightly, 'Is Chelsea playing?'

The big man behind the counter frowned. 'This is Chelsea's stadium.'

Since I already knew that, I repeated my question slowly: 'Is... Chelsea... playing?'

'Only Chelsea play at this stadium,' he snapped.

'Got it. How much is one ticket?'

'You want to attend Sunday's match. And you're not a member.'

It was not a question. He shooed me away, obviously affronted at a causal tourist's effrontery in assuming that a ticket at these revered grounds would be readily available on the eve of a momentous Premier League match.

But later, I managed to get a ticket from the kindly concierge willing to oblige hotel guests. The match was an English Premier League fixture between Chelsea and Manchester City. Sitting among Chelsea fans from London, English counties, Germany, Malta, Boston, and Texas, each group proclaiming its proud affinity with the club by exhibiting banners like 'The Boston Blues', I experienced football fever first-hand. Next to me was a Chelsea fan of forty years, the passion inherited from his father and passed on to his son, who sat next to him, proudly wearing the Chelsea jersey.

The stadium was packed, the atmosphere merry, and the fans noisy. The cheering was continuous and reached thunderous levels on the two occasions that Chelsea scored. It was a heady experience.

On Monday, before our meeting, our group of staid bankers was taken on a stadium tour by an ardent Chelsea fan doubling as guide. Her voice quivering with emotion, she related the history of the club exhaustively, including details like the name of the pub where the club was formed (Rising Sun, now The Butcher's Hook) and the debate about its name (between 'Chelsea' and 'Kensington'). When she told us that Chelsea team never trained at this stadium or the gym next door, preferring their quieter training ground in Surrey, I felt particularly good about the £20 I had not spent.

The highlight of the tour was the changing rooms for the two teams. One is a Spartan affair designed for discomfort, with lockers at floor level and the tactic board hidden by the door whenever it is open, which—as a precaution against fire—is always. The other is a statement of luxury, with gleaming massage tables, individual lockers with the players' jerseys hanging outside, shower rooms fit for kings and a separate hi-tech tactics room. I trust the reader to figure out which room is reserved for the home team and which for the visitors.

I left the stadium recalling an anonymous poet's words:

The love of a beautiful, fair maid,
The love of a staunch, true man,
The love of a baby unafraid,
Have all existed since life began.
But the greatest love—the love of loves—
Greater than that of a mother,
Is the tender, passionate and infinite love,
Of one drunken bum for another.

Eloquently put, but I had just witnessed a love even more tender and passionate—that of a football fan for his club.

The intrepid explorer

Intrepid explorers set off on missions of enormous magnitude with no guarantee of success. On my last day in London, I set off on just such an adventure: to spend the afternoon at the Wimbledon tennis championships before catching my flight back to New York that night. I had no idea if I could get tickets by just landing up at the gate. But Edmund Hillary and Tenzing Norgay probably had no idea of how they would navigate each slippery slope on their climb to Mount Everest. If they didn't let uncertainty dilute their desire, I wouldn't either. Squaring my shoulders, I approached the hotel concierge; unfortunately it was not the same kindly gentleman who had got me the Chelsea match tickets.

'You know Wimbledon?' He stared back stonily, so I elaborated: 'The place they play tennis…' I swung my hand back and played an imaginary forehand stroke, which came out so gracefully that I started demonstrating a one-handed backhand slice, but he stopped me by raising *his* hand.

'*Everyone* knows Wimbledon,' he said coldly, his look implying affront at my insinuation that he lacked such basic knowledge. I apologized and asked him the best way to get to Wimbledon.

'Tube,' he barked and gave me the tube map, invariably at arm's reach anywhere in London. 'But you'll have to lug your suitcase along. There are no luggage storage facilities at tube stations.'

I felt a sharp pang of regret. If I'd brought my tennis bag, I could have carried it around Wimbledon like a professional. Who knows? I might have been mistaken for a player. Perhaps I'd have been asked for an autograph. How would I respond? 'Sorry, I'm a spectator like you?' Or would it be more polite to comply modestly? Should I sign it simply 'Jags' or 'Hi Angela, Wishing you every success in life—Jags Srinivasan'? Would they expect memorabilia, like a wrist band? I wasn't carrying one—should I keep a pair of socks handy?

'Will you take the tube?' The concierge interrupted my happy thoughts.

I told him I wasn't keen on lugging a suitcase all over Wimbledon. He suggested I rent a car, which I could return at the airport as Wimbledon was on the way.

'Brilliant—you're a genius!' I cried.

His good humour restored, he helped me find a taxi. I asked him how far the Avis office was.

'Just three miles away, sir.'

'How long will it take?' I asked, but he had closed the door and stepped back. After crawling forward a few metres, the taxi stopped at a signal and waited there so long I could have gone back and asked him the question again—and at the same time, chatted with him about his family, the weather and the shocking price of onions—and still come back before it moved.

***

I reached Avis ninety minutes later. The paperwork took fifteen minutes and the car's GPS took another fifteen to locate itself. I started my drive at 4.15 pm at a glacial pace, with bicycles and brisk walkers overtaking me. When I stopped at the first signal, six cars were ahead. But the signal turned green so briefly, only two got through. I had to wait for four signal changes, only to get stuck again a few metres ahead. At 4.45 pm I could still see the Avis office in my rear-view mirror.

I inched along, the GPS system directing me with infinite patience. Suddenly at 6.30 pm, the surroundings looked familiar. I was excited. Was I nearing Wimbledon and recognizing the area from what I'd seen over the years on television? What was this bridge I was crossing—it looked so familiar? Then the cruel truth hit me. It was the Stamford Bridge, the one that Chelsea had appropriated for its stadium name. I was back at the hotel I had just vacated!

If, after three weeks of arduous climbing, Hillary and Norgay had found themselves back in base camp, they may have simply shrugged and set off again. But I was made of less spunky steel. Parking the car at the hotel, I requested the concierge to have it returned to Avis on my behalf (£20 extra): I'd take the tube to Paddington and from there, the Heathrow Express to the airport (another £15).

'But you wanted to watch Wimbledon, sir!' the good man said.

'I don't need to leave for another two hours,' I said. 'I'll catch it on television at the hotel bar.'

Exiting the bank

In the last month I had thought a lot about my future and decided to go back to Singapore. For one, I missed the place: driving on the correct side of the road—and being able to get to most places by driving for only 20 minutes—eating *idly-sambhar* in Little India, and buying Dabur Hair Oil in Mustafa whenever I needed to (which was becoming less and less, just like my hair). I was missing Vidya and the kids too. Of course I could have lugged them all the way to the USA too but, and this was the nub of the issue, I realized that banking was not my real calling.

It was customary for me to meet Rick Hamilton, CEO of Anytime Bank every Monday morning if we were both in town, 'to chew the fat', as Hamilton would say. He had brought me into Anytime Bank to inject a dose of marketing into his money-making institution. Not only did I re-design their marketing campaign, but I also sat in Hamilton's key meetings to understand the inner goings-on of the bank. We would exchange notes during these Monday meetings and plan the activity for the coming few days.

So as I walked into his august office on this bright Monday morning, I was wondering how I could veer the conversation to my resignation.

'So, Jags,' said Hamilton, getting up and directing me to his comfortable sofa at one corner of his spacious, elegant office. He sat down across from me. 'Ready to leave us, eh?'

As I stared at him with mouth open, he continued: 'How did I know?' He laughed. 'Elementary, my dear Jags. It's not for nothing that I'm CEO here. You've done a great job in projecting a better image of Anytime Bank to the public. The PR folks tell me our ratings have consistently been climbing since we adopted your new marketing campaign. But within a few weeks of your joining, I knew you were not cut out for banking. I could feel it here.' He poked himself in his chest.

'How?' I was shocked. I had displayed only unbridled zeal for banking to him.

'Well, you've been enthusiastic whenever we talk about banking or your job, but over coffee, when the topic turns to our personal hobbies, you seem to get bored.'

'No!' I cried. 'I play golf too… and talk animatedly about it afterwards.'

'Sure you do,' said Hamilton. 'But golf is only a secondary pastime for a banker. Before we continue, what will you have to drink?'

'Coffee will be fine.'

'Coffee?' He snorted. 'On the day you announce you're leaving? Of course not! I meant bourbon or scotch?' He got up and moved to the stylish cabinet where he kept his drinks.

'It's when we talk about the share market that you tune out,' said Hamilton, when we were seated with glasses of bourbon in front of us.

'Yes, I don't invest in shares,' I said.

'You're the only banker I know who doesn't. And who also doesn't invest in real estate.'

'Ah, that's where you're wrong!' I said, glad to poke a hole in his smugness. 'I'm into real estate. I own the condominium in Singapore that we stay in.'

'That's buying a home, which every idiot does in the USA!' said Hamilton with a dismissive thump of the coffee table. 'That's not investing in real estate! Have you bought any property here in New York?'

I shook my head.

'Exactly!' said Hamilton. 'There were other signs that told me your heart was not in it. I knew your six-month contract is about to end and you can exit with a solid bonus. So when I saw you enter the office today looking apprehensive, I immediately knew and asked you if you're quitting.'

'Oh, it was that simple,' I said. Then, seeing the frown of annoyance on his forehead, I reworded my statement. 'By which I mean that you made a complex deduction look childishly simple.'

Frown turned to guffaw. 'Ha! Ha! You bet I did!' he said, gulping down the last few ounces of his drink. 'Another drink?'

I shook my head. He walked over, filled his own glass and sat down again.

'We'll miss you, Jags. Cheers!'

'Cheers!' I said. We touched glasses and took a sip.

'When do you plan to go back to Singapore?' asked Hamilton.

'In a couple of weeks,' I said, 'if that's okay with you.' He nodded.

'And what do you plan to do next in your career?'

'I'm not sure,' I said.

'But you will not make a living out of the stock market, eh?' he said, with a guffaw.

'No,' I said, 'I'm pretty sure of that. Nor will I become a real estate tycoon.'

'Ha, ha, ha!' he roared. 'That's so funny, it calls for a drink.' He quickly downed his drink. 'Where's your glass?'

Hubby the handyman

I WAS BACK IN SINGAPORE, HAVING quit banking and New York, feeling relaxed and happy during this calm lull between jobs. My wife and I were visiting my cousin who had recently moved here from Chennai. I noticed my cousin's living room cupboard door was flapping outwards at an angle, supported only by its lower hinge.

'I'm waiting for my husband to return,' my cousin said.

'Oh, he has the handyman's number?' I asked.

'No, Ashok will fix it himself—he is very good with his hands. You should see his toolkit!'

'I can fix things too,' I told my wife on our way home. I had noticed her sharp intake of breath when my cousin had spoken.

'No need,' she said, 'Everyone's good at different things. Ashok is good at fixing things. You're good at... er... well, other stuff.'

Ashok's secret was obviously his toolkit. I had to buy one.

'Please give me one normal toolkit for fixing things in the house,' I briskly instructed the do-it-yourself store salesman.

He said this didn't exist. People simply bought the specific tools they needed.

'Please tell me what *I* need,' I said.

The good man put together spanners, screw drivers, pliers, adjustable wrench, hammer, rubber-headed mallet, super-glue, and hack-saw.

'For complex jobs, people buy an electric drill, sir.' He looked at me doubtfully.

I took the hint. 'No, I'll warm up with these; then come back for more elaborate stuff.'

Putting the toolkit firmly on the dining table, I announced: 'I'm ready.'

'Oh,' my wife said dully, without clapping her hands in girlish glee.

'What needs fixing?' I said.

'Nothing. Have some tea.'

I was having none of this prevarication.

'This guest bathroom door latch is giving trouble, right?' I said, 'I'll fix that.'

'No!' she cried, 'Achai'—our handyman—'said we need a new one.'

'Achai will dismantle it, purchase a new one, then come back to fix it, charging us for two visits *and* the new latch. Instead, *I'll* dismantle it and buy a new one. Achai can simply fix it.'

'But *can* you dismantle it?'

I bristled. 'Yes. I have a toolkit.'

The round knobs of the latch came off easily, but the circular base wouldn't budge. The wrench kept slipping. Finally, by inserting the screwdriver underneath and banging on its other end with the mallet, I wrenched it out.

'You've ruined the door!' cried my wife.

'It's a scratch. I'll paint it later.' I moved towards the door to curtail further whining, 'I'm buying a new latch.'

'Sliding the bookmark into the slot is not working? Why not try the full book this time?'

***

When he came home later, Achai frowned.

'Very bad latch, lah,' he said, 'May become jam. Next time I buy. I charge $20 to fix it now'—I gave my wife a see-how-I-saved-$30 look—'and $40 to paint door. Badly scratched.'

'I'll paint it,' I said coldly.

My wife requested me to check the post. When I returned, Achai had fixed the latch... and was painting the door.

'Have some tea,' my wife said.

I magnanimously acquiesced since I wasn't 100 percent sure I could have done the painting with finesse.

***

Two months later, the bathroom door wouldn't open.

'It's jammed, just like Achai said,' my wife said.

'It's the curse of the Achai,' I said.

'Or the inferior latch you purchased.'

Ignoring the slur, I took out my toolkit. But the latch wouldn't budge though I tried the pliers, hammer, wrench...

'You haven't tried the mallet,' said my wife.

I had once observed a handyman open a jammed door by sliding a card in the gap between door and wall; with a click, the door had opened. I slid my best bookmark into the gap and pushed. It got stuck. No click.

'Why not try the full book this time?'

I could feel my wife's breath on my neck. How can an artist perform under such close scrutiny? Would Picasso have produced his paintings if his wife had stood behind him suggesting which brush he use?

At this moment, our cleaning lady was passing by.

'Door jammed?' she asked. She calmly picked up the large screwdriver, inserted it into the slot in the middle of the knob—a slot I had somehow missed noticing—and turned it sharply. With a click, the door opened.

'See that?!' my wife asked in amazement.

'Yes!' I said, 'I'm shocked too. She took my screwdriver without even asking me.'

'Why don't you gift her the toolkit?'

I refused to stoop low and respond to her patently mean-spirited remark.

The guilty party

SITTING IN OUR SINGAPORE APARTMENT balcony, I watched the setting sun cast an orange glow in the sky. Tall apartments cast long shadows across the road. A scorching day was cooling down—by Singapore standards, which means I felt like a medium-rare steak as opposed to one well-done. A light breeze, bringing with it the citrus aroma of fresh lime that I imagined was being squeezed into a neighbour's gin and tonic, helped sustain the illusion of coolness. Amidst the rumble of traffic, I could hear the strains of a rock band (thankfully faint) and, every now and then, the *thump* of a tennis ball in the court below.

It was another beautiful evening during my happy no-job-to-grind-out period. I felt good. I stretched my legs, breathed in deeply and took a sip of tea.

At this point my wife walked into the balcony and stood in front of me. Such was my state of contentment that, even though she was blocking the view of the skyline, I did not baulk.

'Hello, hello, hello!' I said, 'Beautiful evening, no?'

'Well?' she said.

The word 'well', if uttered in a soft tone and accompanied by a smile, can be engaging. Unfortunately my wife did not employ this method—her tone was sharp, her face was illuminated with a frown and her hands were on her hips.

My immediate reaction was that I had done something wrong, but, still feeling mellow and optimistic, I simply smiled.

'Well, what do you have to say for yourself?' she demanded.

My optimism was vanishing and I suspect my smile was turning goofy.

'What day is it?' she asked.

'Friday,' I replied immediately, thinking that was easy... but perhaps too easy to be right.

I was right. The answer was wrong.

'I mean, what's the date?' she snapped.

'The second,' I said.

'of...?' Her voice was menacingly low.

'December,' I said. Then realization dawned. 'Happy Anniversary!'

I tried to bring a note of effervescence into my voice but it was difficult at such short notice.

'How could you forget?' she said, 'We've been married for so many years.'

'That's why,' I came back quickly, thinking on my feet. 'After all, it has been such a long time.'

Thinking on one's feet has its drawbacks, like for example, thinking like an ass. As I said it, I realized that as excuses go, this one wouldn't travel far. Then I suddenly remembered that *she* hadn't wished *me* in the morning. After all, if she had wished me, I would have definitely remembered the date and wished her right back...and we wouldn't be in this uncomfortable position.

I decided to pursue this tack.

'But you forgot too!' I said, 'Yes, oh yes, you forgot too. And now, you're trying to palm off the blame on me when all along...'

'Forgot?' She rudely interrupted me. 'Our wedding anniversary? Me?!'—I think it should have been 'I' but this didn't seem the time to point it out—'How can you even *think* I forgot? I bought this card for you a fortnight ago.'

She pushed a card forcefully into my hand. I opened it—it was nice.

'Thanks,' I murmured, 'I love you too. But why didn't you give it to me this morning?'

'Because last year you forgot to buy me a card but you wished me so sweetly and then we had such a lovely day that I was happy. But later I started thinking, 'Did he forget the card or the anniversary itself?' So this year, I decided to wait and test you.'

I was staggered at her deviousness. She *actually* tested me! I can imagine testing a newcomer you married last month to size him up. But to test a veteran you had been married to for years was outrageous. However, it was she who was looking outraged. I decided to adopt an aggressive stance. I believe I was thinking on my feet again.

'I'm not sure I believe you,' I said coldly. 'Maybe you wished me first last year or maybe I wished you first. A year has passed and it's all murky in my memory. But this year, maybe we *both* forgot; then you remembered during the day and quickly bought the card. What do you say to that?'

'I say, look at this.' She flung a piece of paper on my face. Intrigued, I opened it. It was the receipt for the card... dated two weeks ago. I was shocked at this added proof of the woman's cunning: actually retaining the receipt for a greeting card. How low could she stoop? Words failed me, which was probably for the best.

'And if you'd like to call Original Sin,' she continued, 'you'll find that a table for four has been reserved for 7.30 pm. I did that yesterday. You can check that as well. You would have of course forgotten, but your cousin and her husband are joining us. To remind you, Lata is your cousin; she is married to Ashok—they have two children; the elder, Rahul, goes...'

Once on a sarcastic roll, my wife can go on for a while, but we were luckily interrupted by the phone. It was my cousin calling to wish us and confirm the dinner arrangement.

After much apology (on my part), we went out for dinner. On the whole the evening went well. And therefore, the anniversary ended well. Of course, in my case, it had also started well—except that at that time, I did not know it was my anniversary.

I resolved to remember it next year. And who knows? Maybe I will. But the important question for you, gentle reader, is: which spouse is guilty of the bigger crime—the one who forgets an anniversary or the one who remembers but lays a trap for the other (the one who forgets)?

Been there, done that

'I'M NOT SURE,' I SAID to my wife two weeks later in Singapore.

She had asked the same question Rick Hamilton had put to me a few weeks ago: 'What do you plan to do next in your career?'

'At first I thought I'd go back into marketing in the consumer goods industry.' I said. 'I could probably find something in Gronollers itself. But I feel I've been there, done that. I feel the same way about the advertising agency job.'

'I know what you mean,' said Vidya. 'On her recent visit, when my aunt Ammukutty wanted me to accompany her to the Singapore museum, I told her to go alone. I've been there, done that, I said.'

'Exactly!' I said. Then I got a doubt. 'Were you being sarcastic?'

She assured me she was. 'People don't look for the same novelty in their careers as they do in their tourism experiences.'

'That may be true,' I said, 'but it's just that the passion for marketing and advertising seems to have evaporated,' I explained.

'And that passion never existed for consultancy,' said Vidya.

'Yes and No,' I said, employing the famous cliché used often in the profession we were discussing. 'I never had a raging passion for it but I'm thinking I can start a marketing consultancy on my own.'

'Why?' she asked.

I frowned. 'Why not?!'

'Jags,' she said patiently. 'I'm not asking you why you want to try pistachio ice cream instead of your usual chocolate flavour. You'll be investing time and money setting up your own business. So why start a marketing consultancy when you don't have a passion for consultancy?'

'You're right,' I said. 'Maybe I should start something else, like a restaurant? And by the way, I like pistachio ice cream too,' I added, to set the record straight.

'Good. But why would you want to start a restaurant!?'

'Because it's a very trendy thing to do right now,' I said. 'People from different career backgrounds have started restaurants and done well. Take Brijnath Pandey. He left Deutsche Bank last year to open *Kaveri Kitchen* and it's a hit. We ourselves have gone there thrice.'

'Since he was a child,' said Vidya, 'Pandey has had a passion for cooking, not just eating, like some people I know.'

I wondered why she was suddenly introducing other people into this conversation, but I let it go.

'Do you want to be an entrepreneur?' she asked.

'I don't know,' I said.

'Then the answer is no,' she said firmly. 'A true entrepreneur would know it.'

'I could teach!' I said. 'Many people have done that after interesting careers in the corporate world. Atul Srivastava has been a full-time professor at NUS since he quit Mount Fuji Electronics in 2006. He was telling me…'

'Do you enjoy teaching?' Vidya asked.

I thought about it. 'Yes, I do. I've enjoyed training new recruits in Gronollers in small groups, for example and my FYI (formal yet informal) sessions, where I imparted wisdom on a one-on-one basis, were fun too.'

'That's not quite the same as teaching a class of university students day in day out, is it?'

Well, when she put it like that… I shook my head.

She took my hand in hers and continued in a softer tone. 'Listen, Jags, we're not hard up for money, are we? We own this house. And we have the generous bonus from Anytime. Right?'

I nodded.

'So there's no hurry to jump into something,' she said. 'Look back, Jags.'

I turned around.

'No, not behind you. I mean look back at your *life*. You did Engineering without any interest in the subject, right?'

I nodded.

'Then you joined Kasiram Motors without really wanting to.'

'Yes!' I said. 'But that was Professor Wakefield's fault! He made me…'

'You can't blame Wakefield,' she said. 'You had no clue what you wanted, right?'

I nodded.

'Then,' she continued, 'you joined IIMA.'

'That I wanted to do!' I cried.

'Yes, I grant you that,' she said with a smile. 'And I'm glad you did—or we wouldn't have met! And you did enjoy your summer internship in marketing.'

'I've flitted from point A to point B; from point B to point C; from point C to point D; from...'

I nodded. I was glad we were discussing the happier part of my life history.

'But despite this,' Vidya continued, 'you chose consultancy because it was more popular!'

It looked like we were exiting the happy part of my life history rapidly. I nodded again.

'Then you tried a stint in advertising, got back into marketing and seemed to be enjoying it, when you suddenly jumped into banking for no real reason except that you got an opportunity to do so.'

I nodded some more. My neck muscles were getting a good workout.

'Think back on your life's experiences, Jags.'

I stopped nodding and began thinking.

'You know,' I said after a few moments, 'you're right. It's seems I've flitted from point A to point B; from point B to point C; from point C to point D; from…'

'I get the point,' she said. 'Go on.'

'I can remember almost every incident in this chequered career,' I said. 'I can also remember all the things in between: courting you, our marriage, having our kids and bringing them up, adventures while traveling—on holiday and on work—and all the people I've met.'

I sat silently, letting the memories play in my mind. Vidya waited quietly too.

'You know,' I said after a few minutes. 'If I sat down for the next six months doing nothing else, I could probably write a book about all this stuff.'

'Well, why don't you?' she said.

A Note on the Author

Paddy Rangappa graduated from IIM Ahmedabad 25 years ago and has been working in marketing since then. He is married with two children. He writes in his spare time and has had a regular bi-weekly humour column in *DNA* for the last three years. *Been There Bungled That* is his first book.